PANCAKES FOR ROGER

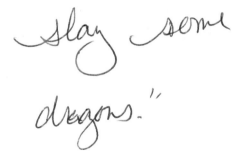

"Be fierce &
slay some
dragons."

FOR ROGER

A MENTORSHIP GUIDE FOR
SLAYING DRAGONS

SUSAN L. COMBS

LIONCREST
PUBLISHING

PANCAKES FOR ROGER

A Mentorship Guide for Slaying Dragons

ISBN 978-1-5445-2839-7 *Hardcover*
      978-1-5445-2840-3 *Paperback*
      978-1-5445-2841-0 *Ebook*

To Josephine, Genevieve, Graham, Weston, and Elliott. Whether you need a hug, a pep talk, a reality check, lunch money, bail money, or a kick in the ass, I got you for life. Go blaze your own trails, slay some dragons, and be tenacious. You are the future.

In loving memory of Major General Roger E. Combs

1945-2018

CONTENTS

PART THREE: FAMILY

PART FOUR: CAREER

Before we start, I want to apologize to my mom for using the F-word and cursing a time or two in this book. My friend Juli tells me I get one F-word a week. My friend Kris says that I live in New York City, so I should get one a day. Either way...sorry, Mom.

INTRODUCTION

"I WANT PANCAKES FOR BREAKFAST," MY DAD SAID AS
he sat at the kitchen table, setting up his placemat, looking
up at me expectantly. We were in my childhood home in
King City, Missouri, a town of just over 1,000. A town that
shaped me, but not nearly as much as the man in front of
me had.

My father was the strongest person I'd ever known: a combat
helicopter pilot, a judge, a Two-Star General, a leader in the
community, a loving husband, the *best* dad, and my go-to
person and role model since day one. This same man was
diagnosed with Agent Orange–related throat cancer in 2008,
and on that late-summer morning ten years later, he was
home on hospice with oxygen and a feeding tube. He'd literally gone to war once in his life before, and now his final
battle was almost over.

Before he got really sick, my dad was known to inject coffee into his feeding tube. I have a picture of him with the coffee and a wry smile. I even saw him put some alcohol in one time. I figured, *Have whatever you want, buddy. You earned it.*

But those times had passed, and his condition had worsened. It was shattering watching my dad's physical decline, especially depending on how he was feeling. He was used to being the go-to person and taking care of everyone else, so it was hard for him to ask for help. My dad and I related and worked together well for his care because I thought about what I would want in his situation to preserve my dignity and independence. I talked to him like a person and explained how allowing help for himself also helped give my mom peace of mind and prevent her feeling guilty if he got hurt, which made sense to him. If we miscalculated the risk, it would affect others, not just him. That says something about his character: he was thinking of others, even as his own clock was winding down.

Because of the tumor growing and subsequent feeding tube, on that morning, pancakes were definitely out of the question. He'd had that tube for over a year, and he'd never once complained about not being able to eat. Occasionally, he'd say something smelled good, but that was it. He was usually content holding my baby niece Josie, or JT as he liked to call her, during meals. And we had the process down to a system: he liked the formula for the tube heated up for exactly fourteen seconds. Feeding tube formula is essentially a protein shake like Ensure. There's a tube down the throat into the stomach. You fill a 50 cc syringe with the formula and then inject it through a connector to the tube. The liquid goes straight to the stomach, which is why my dad always wanted it heated up. It upset his stomach if it was cold.

After my dad was on hospice, our family had a rule: if you got up in the middle of the night, no matter the reason, you had to check on him. He was on oxygen, and he'd move during his sleep and frequently his nasal cannula would come out. We took turns making sure he was getting enough oxygen and adjusting if needed. If his oxygen level became too low, he could become foggy and confused.

That's why that morning, he asked for pancakes despite the feeding tube. He was oxygen deprived.

In his clear mind, he understood that if he choked, we'd be done. When we signed up for hospice, he also signed a DNR—do not resuscitate. We all knew that. That's why I'd moved home from Queens in NYC for basically the entire summer when that time had come...to help my family care for him. To soak up every last second I could get with my dad.

My dad and I were always the type *A*'s in our family, scheduled, regimented people, which I brought with me when I moved back to Missouri for those months he was on hospice. I'd wake up at 5:00 a.m. every morning to go to the gym to do my Dutch Kills CrossFit workout that my coach Dom had posted the night before. Disaster could strike at any time during the day, but at least I would have had an hour for myself. I'd check on him and make sure his oxygen was in place before I left. Then, I'd walk the block to the gym in my hometown, work out, walk back, check on him again, and take a shower. Around then, he'd start to stir. I'd help him with his tube feedings and then get him in his chair, which is where he'd be for the day. I'd get my laptop and work at the coffee table all day, so I was available to help him if he needed anything.

That morning, I came downstairs from that shower when I saw him there, asking for the pancakes. He'd beat me to the table that day.

"Dad, there's nothing more I want to do in this world than give you pancakes, but you know you can't have them," I said. I meant it too. He never complained or made any requests, so it just broke my heart that I couldn't give him the one thing he wanted. "If you choke, we're done. And I don't think we're ready to be done yet."

"Oh yes I can have them," he said. "Matt said I could."

Matt, my brother, is a nurse, and he was a huge part of

the team taking care of my father. He wasn't there that morning, though, and I knew he didn't give that kind of permission.

"Stay there at the table," I told Dad. "Let me see what I can do."

I walked over to the microwave and heated up his formula. Fourteen seconds, on the dot. Then, I sat it down in front of him on the placemat, in between the silverware he'd so neatly set up.

"What's that?"

"That's your syrup," I told him, trying to keep my voice direct and playful in a way that was always "our way." But maybe it cracked just a little.

I could tell his oxygen levels were improving, and he understood.

He stared up at me then, looking resigned and tired. But his eyes still crinkled with the signs of a smile.

"Okay."

A little over a month later, on August 22nd, 2018, Dad would be done fighting.

Toward the end, Dad was suffering so much that I'd say a prayer when I entered his room that he'd be asleep and gone. He wasn't himself anymore. Then, sometimes he'd have some decent days where his oxygen was up and he was a little more interactive. His last "excursion" was to his brother's funeral three weeks before his own passing. It was good for his nieces and nephews to see him. We didn't know if it was safe to let him attend, but the service was for his brother, and they'd been extremely close.

I wasn't able to give him the pancakes he wanted that day, but what I can do is make damn sure his memory lives on. That's why you're reading this book.

#PANCAKESFORROGER

When I came back to New York after my dad passed, I remember sitting in the airport and coming across a quote that would be meaningful later: "Trust the wait. Embrace the uncertainty. Enjoy the beauty of becoming. When nothing is certain, anything is possible." Later in this book—which contains vignettes, advice, and lessons from my father and many other influential people in my life, little stories and scenes that have stuck with me through all my years that I believe can add some value to yours—I'll share the airport story with you.

I have shared the pancake story with many people because

I know the message goes beyond what happened at that kitchen table. I want people to know it's the little things in life that make a huge impact. Take the time to enjoy little things, like pancakes, that you take for granted. Someday, you may not be able to. It's a simple message to hear, but it's a hard one to internalize, especially in our busy lives.

When I arrived back in NYC, I took a day off of work, and my husband suggested we go get some pancakes. He snapped a photo, and I posted it with the story. This is where #PancakesForRoger started.

Over the next few months, I started receiving pictures from people who said they'd had pancakes and thought about my dad. I still get text messages saying people can't have pancakes without thinking about him. His birthday is February 22nd, so the first one after he passed, I decided we could use #PancakesForRoger to help get some recognition for the University of Missouri School of Law Veterans Clinic, which trains law students to help veterans and their families navigate the complex VA claims system and essentially builds a network of ambassadors for veterans across the US.

The mission of the Veterans Clinic is important to our country for obvious reasons. Those who have given all deserve to be taken care of. In a time of increasing divisiveness in our country, I don't know anyone who would argue that simple fact. And the Veterans Clinic helps people do that.

Besides that, the mission is important to me and my family on a personal level. Before my dad went to Vietnam, he had completed a semester of law school. Because he had a BS, he was able to go through Officer Candidates School (OCS) and start his military career as a Second Lieutenant in the Marine Corps and a combat helicopter pilot. My mom didn't want to be an active duty military wife, so he went on reserve duty and resumed law school.

Though he was actually activated to be deployed during Desert Storm, the Air Force deemed it more important for him to be home during that time because my brother had cancer*—another story I'll share with you in this book, also filled with lessons. Just because he didn't redeploy didn't mean Dad stopped caring. He still liked to go visit the veterans. He was also quick to point out that people were patriotic and pro-military during Desert Storm, but many Vietnam veterans did not have a good homecoming. In the 1990s, people tied yellow ribbons around trees in their front yards. But when Dad came home, veterans like him got spat on.

Dad often shared that he would go register for classes in a wig to cover up the military crew cut because he didn't want to be heckled. In law school, he found more of his tribe, being surrounded by classmates and professors who also

---

* Patricia Knapp went in my father's place and served during this time. Our family will always be grateful to her.

served. He talked about their gatherings with pizza, beer, and war stories. He valued those peer-to-peer mentors who had experienced similar journeys.

My brother, Mom, and I agreed that Dad would want people to make donations to the Veterans Clinic in lieu of sending flowers after his passing. Our family became integrated into that system for that and another big reason. My dad lived below his means—another thing he taught me that I'll share with you later—so there was enough money to provide for my mother *and* to set up an endowment scholarship for veterans who want to go to the University of Missouri School of Law. The first recipient, Alex, is in his final year at the time of this writing, and he's currently in the National Guard. He also works at the Veterans Clinic. That personal connection has been great for us. We met him for the first time at a #PancakesForRoger breakfast at the University of Missouri, and I'll never forget it.

People have been after me to write a book for a while because I so often share my "dadisms," so I thought there was no better way to honor my dad and help veterans than by writing *Pancakes for Roger* and donating part of the proceeds to the Veterans Clinic to help further their mission to help veterans and their families navigate the VA system and appeals process. This work is particularly important because VA claims take, on average, seven years to process. I don't need to tell you that is unacceptable.

My dad's claim took three years, which we thought was a long time...but the clinic thought his experience was incredible. As I mentioned, he was both a Two-Star General and a judge, so he knew how to write and advocate for himself. One in fourteen of our veterans actually pass away during the process, waiting for what is owed to them. By helping the Veterans Clinic, we are paying tribute to my dad while also helping others benefit from his knowledge and experience. That little oxygen-deprived moment over pancakes had a ripple effect we couldn't have realized at the time.

A portion of the proceeds from the sale of this book benefits the University of Missouri School of Law Veterans Clinic to further their mission to help veterans and their families navigate the VA claims and appeals process.

I own an insurance brokerage in New York, and my company now aligns with a charity every year. In February, we encourage people to go have pancakes and post a picture with the hashtag. For every picture posted, we donate to the Veterans Clinic. The first time, we threw the idea together and received about 100 pictures. Since then, the tradition has taken off, and it's been really fun. Kids get involved, and this past year, people in all fifty states and fourteen different countries participated. People in the military, veterans, the American Legion, and others have pancake breakfasts now. The first year we saw maybe a couple hundred pictures across our social media platforms, but this past year, there were more than 1,000. We gave awards for the most creative pancake, the school spirit pancake, and other contributions. It's great and feels like part of his legacy.

Pancakes have become a special ritual for my family too. We'll eat them in his memory. He had two funerals, one at our local funeral home and one at Arlington National Cemetery, and after his full military service at Arlington, we invited our close family and friend circles to come to the house we rented the following morning for a big pancake breakfast. Those rituals are particularly important to me living in New York City, since my in-laws are here but not my immediate family. I want to hold on to the traditions and rituals that remind me of my family and of growing up.

So many people tell me they had pancakes and thought about my dad, and I can't tell you how much those stories make me smile. People tell me how he helped them or share other stories about him, and it helps keep me going.

MY HOPE FOR YOU

I have a breadth of life experience having grown up in the rural Midwest and then moved to New York City, and I've been incredibly lucky over the years. I have a family that loves me. I got a full ride to college. I've hustled my ass off in my industry and have a successful company. I married the love of my life. I have my health. In short, I look really good on paper.

But I didn't get here alone. Nobody gets anywhere alone. In fact, my greatest accomplishment is that I'm a mini–Roger Combs, and that would be my greatest accomplishment even if none of the things I said in that last paragraph were true.

I'd much rather be remembered as a badass who is a good person and helps people when they need it. My dad was an example of that. He was good when no one was watching. Everything I've learned about him after he passed has cemented that legacy even further.

The day after my dad died, in fact, my brother Matt went down to the post office to pick up the mail for my mom. The postmaster started talking about how amazing our dad was. Once, they said, my mom had noticed the AC was out at the post office, and she told my dad when she returned home. Not ten minutes later, my dad came by with bottled water and a fan.

Three years after my dad died, a man gifted my mom a beautiful wooden cross he'd made just because my dad was a good, memorable man who'd helped him. I once talked to a woman whom my dad had helped with custody issues when she was a little girl, and she said he made her feel safe when no one else would. He let kids come into his chambers and would show them pictures of his own kids. He'd have honest conversations with kids to see what they wanted and what would make them feel safe. A man I went to school with said he was going down the wrong path, and my dad gave him a second chance by having a "come to Jesus" conversation and suspending his sentence. He said he couldn't thank my dad, so he wanted to thank me.

Seeing my dad's legacy makes me want to do nice things. I want people to have good memories and gratitude for me when I'm no longer here. I don't need an award, a billboard, or recognition. I just want to live by the golden rule.

I've been blessed with so many meaningful and important mentors in this life, and they've helped me slay a hell of a lot of dragons. From them, I've gained perspective and motivation. I know my fellow women are often brilliant multi-taskers and take care of so many people, but sometimes we need to be taken care of too. And there's strength in seeking that out. I know you're that strong already because you recognized that and picked up this book.

If you don't have a mentor in your life just yet, I invite this book to be that for you until you can find someone. And, maybe, even after you find someone.

WHAT TO EXPECT IN THIS BOOK

You don't have to have a military connection to care about #PancakesForRoger. If you've ever lost someone or even just experienced an accident or hardship, you know the world can change in the blink of an eye.

You also don't have to have lost a parent or suffered a huge personal loss to care about the lessons in this book. We all need reminders to stop and be present. We all need advice at times—myself most certainly included.

In fact, I'll shoot you straight, now and always. Not every vignette in this book is for everyone, and not all advice will speak to you specifically in terms of where you are in life. *That's okay.* When my brother was born, my uncle Joe told my mom, "You're going to get a lot of advice. Take what you want, and throw out the rest."

This is permission—though you certainly don't need it—to do the same. I've been around the block, and I know that what you need to do next depends on where you are in your life and what you see coming next. Logistically, to help you choose your guideposts and where to start, the lessons and stories in this book are broken down into four parts: Self, Love, Family, and Career.

Do you need to remember to have stretch in your life? Do you need to stay humble as you're climbing? Do you need to have some hard conversations? Do you need to find a peer-to-peer mentor? These are all lessons I've learned and will share with you here, if you are willing to come on the journey with me.

It's about choosing your own adventure—which, uncoincidentally, is where we'll start.

Part One

SELF

CHOOSE YOUR OWN ADVENTURE

I GRADUATED FROM COLLEGE IN 2001 WHEN THERE was a great job market. I had various job offers but set my heart on New York City. I got an apartment and a roommate and had accepted a job in the Marriott at the World Trade Center. Two weeks before, Marriott corporate called to say the position was consolidated, and I could choose between Detroit or New Orleans instead.

Detroit or New Orleans? My mom had pictures of New York on my going-away cake. My dad had personally taken me to the city during spring break to help me get a feel for such a big move. I was ready for New York, and the rug was pulled out from under me, job-prospect-wise. I was at a crossroads.

I knew those other cities weren't me, and I made the decision to come to New York without a job and see what I could find in May of that year. I interviewed and interviewed and interviewed. I learned about networking. I'm the youngest grandchild, and my cousin Pat who is the oldest grandchild is twenty years older (almost to the day). He introduced me to a friend whose sister was a recruiter in New York. I shared with her that I'd had experience in hospitality, having worked on events for huge music acts in my college career including Bob Dylan, Kenny Rogers, and Destiny's Child. The recruiter suggested I go meet with...wait for it...a payroll company.

Payroll was not sexy, and it was not my dream. But I liked the company. I'd taken a great deal of math as an undergrad and thought I could use those skills by auditing companies. While I was working for the company, they came out with their new product: Workers Compensation. This was my first step into the world of insurance.

What I could have never known was that, by taking that opportunity, I would find the best field for me, start my own business, and end up where I am today. What I also could have never known is that, had the original job not fallen through, I would likely have been working right next door to The World Trade Center on September 11th, 2001.

Instead of being at Ground Zero on that day, I watched the towers fall from our office window on the twenty-ninth floor. I had on high heels, and I waited in a line that stretched a block to buy sneakers, so I could walk across the Queensboro Bridge to get home. I needed to get out of the city—which is what locals refer to as Manhattan—and there were no trains running.

That day turned the whole city of New York into a small town like King City, from my perspective. People were kind. They held the door for each other. It became a different place, and it also became my home. I fell in love with it then. If you were here on that day, you are so interconnected to the city. All the people I worked with still reach out to each other every anniversary. We're connected for life.

Had everything worked out as planned, I might have been dead at twenty-two. My path working out like it did tells me I have some greater purpose—partly to share what I know, partly to leave you with this piece of advice: to follow your gut and not be afraid to choose an adventure that can feel uphill at first.

"DON'T LET YOUR ALLIGATOR MOUTH OVERLOAD YOUR TADPOLE BEHIND."

I ALWAYS HAD A BIG PERSONALITY, EVEN AS A KID. I'M outspoken and say what I think, which can get me into trouble sometimes. My mom told us as kids not to let our alligator mouths overload our tadpole behinds. Similarly, my dad said, "Be aware of the toes you step on today, because they could be connected to the ass you have to kiss tomorrow."

All these sayings point to the same wisdom: know your audience, and be appropriate. That advice can be hard for someone like me who's always been outspoken, but it's also important.

Even if I don't say what I'm thinking, you'll see it on my face. If I think you're full of shit, you pretty much know it. If I don't like you, you pretty much know it, just by how my face looks. That means that from a young age, these sayings have been good reminders for me from time to time whenever I start to get a little bit too big for my britches.

As you move through the world, stay humble and true. Remember your roots and where you're from. Humility is important even as you tap into your own capability. You can be strong and not be a bitch. It's about the delivery. Wonder Woman is a strong, badass woman. She also has the lasso of truth, so her focus stays on doing what's right. You can be strong and fierce while also maintaining credibility and humility.

LEARN TO CONNECT WITH ANYONE

I ONCE WENT OUT FOR A MEAL IN NEW YORK WITH family friends who had their daughter with them. She's a sweet kid and an only child, so she just brought her book and spent the meal reading. Afterward, my husband commented how the experience must have been boring as hell for her. I can see that point of view, but it's also possible to teach your kids to engage.

My parents took me to everything, exposing my brother and me to all kinds of people, which I appreciate more the older I get. We interacted with people from many different walks of life from a very young age, and we weren't allowed to just sit there and be quiet. We were expected to carry on conversations with everyone from generals and dignitaries to dairy farmers and preachers.

As a result, I've inherited from my father the ability to talk to anybody. In this era of technology, it's easy to forget how to have a conversation. People can be great with their written word and shooting off an email. Then, in person, they can turn into what my family calls the "ugly third grader"—so awkward and uncomfortable in their own skin that they can't have a face-to-face conversation. It's important to continually hone social skills for them *and* for adults.

When my father had his retirement party in Missouri, it was an amazing experience because it brought all his circles together: family, church, courthouse, and military. He was very accomplished and has a four-page Wikipedia page, for context. In the military, they called him "Judge," and in the civilian world, they called him "General." He's a big deal, but many people from King City and even our family members didn't realize some of his accomplishments. Some of his colleagues from when he was a Marine Corps helicopter pilot in Vietnam were there, and everyone had different experiences with him to share.

It was so rewarding as his child to see him receive the recognition he deserved.

People outside the military got to see how he was held in high regard and learn about his awards and accolades in a way that felt authentic to who he was. He was the youngest child in his family and never wanted to brag or make anyone feel bad. It's always been amazing to me how he kept a foot in both worlds and balanced his life so beautifully.

My dad was always a humble person. It was great to see him receive the love people were giving him, even though he was a smartass by nature with a dry sense of humor. He could zing you in a way you wouldn't realize for a week. But in that moment, I could tell he appreciated the party and was taking it all in.

Though he was humble, what he didn't do was brush the positive attention off. Sometimes when someone gives you a compliment or celebrates your success, it's tempting to minimize it like it's no big deal—especially for women. But do you know what? Our accomplishments *are* a big deal, just like they were for him.

"DRIVE THE CAR."

IF YOU'RE A KID GROWING UP IN THE MIDWEST, YOU get to drive, whether it's going down to turn the water on for the horses or using the tractor to put up hay. Kids drive the tractor or the car with a trailer on it. My dad taught me how to parallel park between a horse trailer and a feed truck on the farm, which is a skill you can't put a price tag on, especially living in New York City today.

When it came time to learn formal highway driving, my dad would always say, "Drive the car." He said you can be the best driver in the world, but you have to worry about the people around you. That meant that no matter what happened, whether you got cut off in traffic or hit an animal or had any number of issues, your priority was always simple: drive the car.

Don't get me wrong; my dad cared about safety. He always told me if someone's in your lane, don't swerve into their lane because then you're likely to have a head-on collision when they come to their senses and correct. He had my brother and me go through defensive driving school because our school didn't have driver's ed. The driving school was what he made minors in his court do as a consequence, but he placed us there electively. I got laughed at in that class one day because they brought out a breathalyzer, and I blew it through the hole like I was trying to blow a bubble. I was the only one in the group who'd never had to take one.

Whenever I was behind the wheel, he'd talk about how I needed to anticipate what other people might do and just *drive the car*. He'd also jerk the steering wheel, and I had to avoid freaking out. If something happened and I needed to pull over, I'd take my foot off the gas, gather myself, and then reenter traffic.

Later in life, after he was diagnosed and treated at the Mayo Clinic, I traveled to Minnesota to help with his care post-surgery and to drive him back to Missouri with my mom. It wasn't a minor surgery; in fact, he looked like an attempted Mob hit. They'd cut him from ear to ear, and he had a trach.

As we were leaving and he slid in the passenger seat, he said, "Now, Suz, I know you are an excellent driver, and we are going to make it just fine, but I just want you to know that if we are in even a minor accident, I'm probably dead."

Talk about white-knuckling it the 350-mile drive that lay ahead! Good thing my General Combs–training took over, and I remembered to "drive the car," and we made it safely home that day.

"Drive the car" is a good metaphor for life and keeping things in perspective. If you get derailed in life, sometimes you need to assess the situation and then get back to driving. Go back to the basics. What do you need to focus on to get going again?

When my dad was on hospice, I kept that advice in mind. The stress associated with hospice was so much. If you know any caregivers, you need to check on them because I can attest to the fact that it's draining. My "drive the car" during that time was setting my intentions in the morning and going to the gym every day. That way, I had something for myself, and the rest of the day, I could give to others.

If my dad's oxygen got low or he got into his meds because he was confused, I'd go back to "drive the car" to come up with a solution. My family assessed the situation and put away all his meds to keep him safe or did what we needed to do.

Sometimes, I think about how my dad learned many of the lessons he ended up teaching my brothers and me, and I often wonder if many of them came from his time as a combat helicopter pilot. When you have people's lives in your hands, you have to keep the mission always in the forefront, shut out the noise, and not let distractions derail you. It's important to keep going even in the face of overwhelming circumstances. Fly the helicopter. Drive the car.

My dad and I both considered worst-case scenarios. In my job in insurance today, I look at the worst-case scenario for living. If you know what that scenario is and realize there's a 90 percent chance it won't happen, then you can better deal with the little bumps along the way. And you know how to keep driving when you hit them.

Women often second-guess ourselves, but sometimes we just have to do a gut check and move forward. Once we make the decision, there's no sense in getting trapped in what-ifs. You might make the wrong decision, but you can learn from it, and those mishaps build your character and make you who you are today. The fear of failure can be paralyzing, so it's important to cultivate confidence in ourselves, our decisions, and our ability to recover. Mistakes are part of your story. Those are the bumps. What you do after you hit them is up to you.

REMEMBER WHERE YOU COME FROM

I GREW UP IN A TOWN WITH 986 PEOPLE. I GRADUATED from a high school class with fifteen kids and then moved to New York City after graduating from the University of Missouri. Even though I've lived in New York for over twenty years now, I've never forgotten where I'm from. I had a wonderful upbringing, a wonderful childhood, and wonderful parents, which not everyone does. Regardless of your experience, I think if you deny yourself your past or say you have regrets, then you're denying yourself your place in the world right now. It's important to remember what made you and shaped you into who you are, for better or worse. If you have a painful past, now you're a survivor—so how can you take your story to somebody else and be an inspiration to them?

There's a line between being braggadocios and sharing your

good news to help or inspire others. I once spoke at a business school in New York. The CFO of a very large computer company was there, a woman probably in her sixties at the time, and I was in my thirties. She said, "Don't roar after the kill." In other words, when you have an accomplishment, you don't have to brag. I was sitting at a table of college students, including one who would become a future employee, Ricarte, when she said this. As I rose from the table to take the stage as the next speaker, I looked at the students at the table and said, "Roar after the freakin' kill because if you don't roar for yourself, nobody else will roar for you."

That said, there's a way to share the information without bragging. You have to give people the opportunity to celebrate you, which is why my company has a Wonder Woman Wednesday campaign (brainchild of my business partner, Colleen)—we want to shine the spotlight on their accomplishments, and sometimes they're not good at shining the spotlight on themselves.

You can break that cycle, starting now.

KNOW YOURSELF

IT'S IMPORTANT TO KNOW YOURSELF. FOR EXAMPLE, I also work in the field of expert witnessing, and it's rewarding because it suits me. I have a sense of wonder and curiosity that I can satisfy by learning about different companies, which is integral to my insurance job. To insure a business, we have to understand the operations, where the product comes from, what the marketing involves, and so on. When I serve as an expert witness, I also get to work with extremely smart people, I get to be creative, and I get to strategize. All those things light me up. This book also satisfies and helps satisfy my creative side.

That's me. It might not be you, and that's part of what makes this world beautiful: our differences.

You've got to understand who you are and what your likes and dislikes are. I know this sounds simple as hell, but how many of us have actually taken the time to sit down and think this way? If you're creative but your job doesn't tap into that impulse, what can you do as a side hustle or a hobby to enrich your life creatively? My business partner Colleen started a podcast called *Try and Stop Me* to help satisfy her creativity. She gets to meet new people and learn about new subjects. She loves her career but was missing a piece that the podcast now helps fill.

It's impossible for one aspect of your life to fulfill everything you need, so seek out different people and pursuits to make a well-rounded life. If you try to make your spouse, a friend, or your career everything to you, you will fail. My husband is my friend and my family, but I also need a larger circle than just him who I can connect with. It's too much pressure for one person to be my everything, just as my career can't fulfill every single desire in my life. If you're in a knowledge-work career and miss physical activity, then add in some manual labor to your life, like gardening or hiking.

The bottom line? Do whatever you need to do to fill your soul.

KEEP F*CKING GOING

AFTER MY DAD PASSED, MANY PEOPLE REACHED OUT
to me on social media or by text message to offer condolences, but what I was surprised by was that the people who gave me the most comfort really weren't the people in my close circle. They were fellow members of "The Club" nobody wants to be in. There was my friend Kacie, who lost her father just a few years before my dad died, and my best friend Kerre, who had lost her father when we were in high school. At the time, that was the closest I'd been to such a loss. These two supported me when I didn't realize I needed it most.

One story in particular that stayed with me was from Kacie. She shared that when her father passed away, she got a bracelet that said, "Conquer." She said she wore it every day the first year to remind herself that even during the toughest times that she was going to conquer her sadness and she would conquer her challenges and live her life to the fullest as her dad wanted her to.

I thought about that story and looked for a piece of jewelry that might serve a similar motivating purpose for me. I found a bracelet that had "Keep f*cking going" inscribed inside, so no one knew it was there unless I showed them. I still wear the bracelet on days I'm feeling vulnerable and need a little help from Dad. But right after he passed, I wore it every single day for a year, and it served as a constant reminder to persevere—even though I felt like I'd been kicked in the gut and wanted to throw in the towel. Some days, I just wanted to sit in my grief, and that bracelet nudged me to show up anyway because that's what my dad did. He experienced significant tragedy in his life but always showed up for other people—and we can too.

EMBRACE UNCERTAINTY

AFTER MY DAD PASSED, I FOUND THIS QUOTE, AND IT touched me deeply: "Trust the wait. Embrace the uncertainty. Enjoy the beauty of becoming. When nothing is certain, anything is possible."

I've always sought out motivational quotes, and though I'm not a very religious person, I drew strength from faith because I felt like I had nothing. I had often prayed, before walking into the room to check on my dad, for him to pass because I knew he was suffering, but after he died, I felt lost. He and I were tremendously close. So, I looked for words that would fill me up. I had great people to support me, but I needed something to believe in. The idea of trusting the wait and anything being possible when nothing is certain spoke to me because I knew my life had forever changed.

I had to trust the process of starting a new journey. My dad's brother Larry had also just passed away, and my cousin Lance told me life would be different, but that doesn't mean it would all be bad. Anyone who has lost a parent is a member of this "Club" and knows the profound change that loss entails.

As I revisited the quote nearly every day in the first year after my dad passed, it helped me keep perspective regarding the changes on the horizon. Even though my dad was gone, I could still believe in myself. I realized I could become a living tribute to the life he lived so well.

I had to move forward knowing I couldn't bring my dad back. I trusted there was so much more left to my story. For me, that means that even though he's not here, I can be part of his living legacy. I can tell people about his life. I had a dad who was good when no one was watching, which has made me want to carry myself the same way in the world. I feel motivated to do random acts of kindness no one will ever know about. I feel like on the other side of my father's death, I'm a much better person. I'm so much more empathetic. I can see people for who they are now and truly feel their pain, which I don't think I did before. Embracing uncertainty was the first step to this growth.

RESCUE YOURSELF

WHEN MY DAD DIED, I WROTE FOR MAGAZINES AND ON social media about my experience, and so many people reached out to say how much my story helped them. That is the purpose of this book too.

One of my favorite quotes by Marcus Aurelius is, "Get active in your own rescue." In looking for quotes, wearing the bracelet, and drawing on the perseverance my father taught me, I was finding ways to actively move through my own grief rather than passively suffering. You can't wait for someone else to save you in your own life. But as my dad used to say, "In order to kick ass, you have to first pick up your own foot."

Some people complain about the same thing over and over, without ever taking a step to change the situation, but I'm not wired that way. Einstein's often-quoted description of insanity is doing the same thing over and over but expecting different results. Sometimes, you have to be your own hero. This can be difficult, especially for women. But we're so much stronger than we realize—and often we don't realize that until we face loss or adversity. In those hard moments, when your impulse can be to look elsewhere, I encourage you to take a moment to be still and feel your own strength. Asking for help is huge and important, but don't forget your biggest advocate is always inside.

I recently saw a post that Cinderella never asked for a prince; she asked for a night off and a dress. Be your own hero.

REMOVE "ONE SIZE FITS ALL" FROM YOUR VOCABULARY

WHEN I WAS SIXTEEN YEARS OLD, WE HOSTED AN exchange student named Anne from Germany. I don't remember what happened, but I got pissed off at her, even though we had and continue to have a great connection (she's become my sister after all, and that's what sisters do). I ended up throwing a milk carton at her in an outburst. My dad took my bedroom door off its hinges as punishment. I knew I could hang the door by myself (I was Roger's daughter after all), and I went into his bedroom to find the pins. I was pretty sure he had put them on his dresser, but I couldn't find them. I tried to sneak back across the floor to my room, but my dad caught me. He stared at me from the bottom of the stairs, pins in hand. I can still hear his voice. "Looking for these, little girl?" He had my number. He anticipated what punishment would work for me and how I'd try to get around it. He knew how I thought because he too would have done the same thing at my age. I apologized and got my door back in a day. Our family was good at resolving issues and moving on rather than pretending nothing happened.

I remember my dad telling me he knew I was devious from when I was four years old. My brother got a pup tent for his birthday, and we were camping out in the front yard. We'd take turns coming into the kitchen and climbing onto a chair to get the Twinkies and candy we weren't allowed to have. Finally, at two in the morning, my dad turned on the light and yelled for us to come inside. He asked if I'd been eating Twinkies, and I said no, even though I had cream all over my face. He said he knew I was going to be like him: not a liar all the time by any means, but someone who thought fast to save their ass.

Once I was backing out of the driveway and knocked against a pickup truck on the curb that belonged to Darryl, a guy who worked at the local auto body shop. I didn't damage it. My dad said I needed to look up the phone number of the prosecuting attorney, provide it to Darryl, and tell him to call Mr. Manring if he decided to press charges. I called, super nervous, and explained what had happened. Thankfully, he said it was no big deal. My dad said if I'd been prosecuted, I would have received ten hours of community service, so he arranged for me to do ten hours of work.

My dad was great at coming up with creative solutions that would teach us in the moment. The approaches that worked on me never would have worked on my brother Matt, and vice versa. Before you try to solve a problem, consider who the players are, and develop your strategy from there to have the biggest impact.

In your adult relationships, it's wise to have the way you handle situations fit both the situation and the person. My dad did a good job of looking at us as individuals, and I carry that into my friendships and connections with my family today.

MOVE THROUGH THE WORLD WITH YOUR EYES WIDE OPEN

ON MY FIRST WORK TRIP AFTER MY DAD PASSED, I WAS in the Austin airport heading back home from speaking at a conference, and I saw a piece of art that resonated with me so much, I bought a copy. It's a photo collage by an artist named Leslie Kell called "One More Day." I'd never had art speak to me, but it pulled me in. It has flowers and a crypt, and in the background, there's a silhouette walking through. The silhouette looks almost identical to my father's before he was sick. I found the artist and emailed her to tell her my experience, and I said I had to have that piece of art.

She said she lost her father before she did the piece, and that experience manifested in the work. I was open to that experience. I'm not usually someone who spends more than

$1,000 on a piece of art, but I needed it. It was my Christmas present to myself, and I look at it and talk to my dad sometimes. It hangs right above my desk in my home office where I did all the writing for this book. Also, in that home office is where an inversion table used to be. I'd needed it in preparation for having two back surgeries in thirteen months.

I'd be upside down, looking at this piece of art, imagining my dad telling me to stop flipping 600-pound tires in my Strongman class at Dutch Kills CrossFit.

Because I was open to signs and things beyond my control, that piece of art and I intersected in the right place at the right time. I believe it's important to stay open to what comes your way. You can miss out because you're staring at your phone or thinking of what you want to say next instead of moving forward with your eyes wide open.

NAVIGATE THE THREE FACETS OF LIFE

WHEN I GOT MY HEART SET ON WORKING IN NEW YORK, my mom told my dad to take me on spring break and show me the worst parts of the city. We experienced a Nor'easter storm, which is almost like a mini hurricane. We were staying on military bases because it was cheap, and I was driving in the storm while my dad told me, "This is going to be your life."

We got on a train from Connecticut to New York. We passed through litter-strewn neighborhoods, and I was smiling from ear to ear. My dad joked with me to talk myself out of it, but I accepted the job in New York—which then dissolved two weeks before it ever started.

My mom fretted about me going, but my dad reminded her I'd been in ROTC, this was how I was awarded that full ride to college. I could have been stationed in Germany or Korea and not come home for three years. Instead, I was just a plane ride away. A while later, I moved back to Kansas City for a few months. I wasn't with the right guy, I hated where I lived, and I was back to selling payroll, which wasn't what I wanted to do. I knew by the second day it was the wrong decision.

Since I moved back to New York for good, my mom has said she'd rather I be far away and have a good relationship than close and miserable.

My dad always said there are three facets to your life: the person you're with, the thing you do for a living, and the place you live. If you can line up three out of three at any given time, you're living a golden life. Two out of three is pretty good. But if you only have one or none, you need to get off your butt and make a change.

"NO STEP FOR A STEPPER"

MY DAD USED TO ALWAYS SAY, "NO STEP FOR A STEP-per." It's a Marines saying meaning, "You got this." Anytime I had a stretch in my life and felt discouraged, he'd say it. They're words of encouragement that I got tattooed on my wrist on his first birthday after he passed.

Look...I talk a good talk, but I need encouragement too. Sometimes the hardest workers need to dig deep within themselves to drive on. My dad always strived for greatness, and I do too. I never half-ass anything. I make mistakes, but nothing's worth doing if you aren't going to do it right. And if it's worth doing, it's no step for a stepper.

SEE THE SIGNS

THE OTHER DAY, I WAS TAKING AN UBER, AND THE driver missed my turnoff, which resulted in a detour that took me miles out of my way. I was extremely annoyed. Then, as the driver made the exit, I noticed the median was covered with sunflowers, which are a sign from my dad. I realized he'd wanted to send me a message, so the detour had a reason.

I'm a big believer in signs. My favorite book is called *Signs: The Secret Language of the Universe* by Laura Lynne Jackson. Not everyone believes in the woo-woo stuff, but I believe in some of it. My friend Angela gave me this book almost exactly a year after my dad passed. The book states that if you ask for signs, you'll get them—but you have to be specific and more importantly, you have to be open.

One of the things that always stood out for me was sunflowers. My dad was a farm boy. My grandmother always planted flowers on my birthday as a tradition. There was a garden across the street from our house that my dad loved.

Once he decided to grow his own birdfeed by planting sunflowers behind the house, but they were atrocious. They were nine feet tall, and my mom thought they were gross, but they made him smile. He'd cut off the heads, dry them, and put them out for the birds in the winter. Whenever I see sunflowers, I think of my dad.

This past summer, everyone in Queens had sunflowers. There was one I walked by every single day I went to the gym. The flower was in a little four-by-two-foot piece of land. I watched it grow for six weeks, and then it just burst open. It was cool to feel the excitement, especially since I talk to my dad in my head a lot when I walk to the gym.

Another sign from my dad is helicopters because he was a helicopter pilot. We also had a song, Crystal Gayle's "Don't It Make My Brown Eyes Blue." My mother has such beautiful blue eyes, and when I was a little girl, I wanted my eyes to look like hers. When I was three or four years old, if you put me in front of a mirror and asked me what color my eyes were, I'd say blue—even though they're about as dark brown as they come. If people tried to tell me my eyes were brown like my dad's, I'd deny it, so he used to sing me the Crystal Gayle song. When we were kids, we had a van with an 8-track, and my tape was Crystal Gayle. My brother's was Karen Carpenter, though he might kill me for telling you that.

After my dad died, I went to a seminar led by the author Laura Lynne Jackson. I attended with my friend Debbie. She was very open to the experience and has a kind of sixth sense about her, so she mentored me and was another part of the "tribe" that helped me so much when my dad first passed. The seminar was on her birthday, about fourteen months after my dad had passed. We talked about different signs. We were supposed to bring something from the person who passed, and then we'd exchange items with a partner and try to read the energy.

The number I had for my dad was forty-five because he was born in 1945. The author encouraged us to be more complex with our signs, so I came up with a purple tiger. My dad's Marine Corp squadron was known as the Purple Foxes, and we both went to University of Missouri—home of the Tigers.

The woman I randomly got matched up with handed me a ring she'd brought, and I said I felt like the person who had worn it was an artist and created something with their hands. Then, I started really looking at the ring. The stone in the center was purple. It had once had five stones, but one was missing, so it was four and then five—like forty-five. As I talked to her, she said it was her grandmother's ring because her grandmother was a jeweler. She told me the stone was called a purple tiger's eye.

I went to Arlington, where my father was interned in the columbarium, after they finished engraving and installing his headstone in December 2019. I was sitting on a nearby bench talking to him, and helicopters were passing overhead. I looked down, and there was a wreath with purple flowers and tiger lilies. My grandparents are buried there too, so I went to see them. Something told me to turn around, and I saw a wreath of sunflowers.

My husband doesn't believe in signs like this, but he's sweet about pointing those connections out for me. In life, sometimes you don't see what's out there unless you're open. I try to be open to seeing these signs of my father. So much in life is connected. You didn't make the sunrise, and I didn't either. There's more to the universe than we perfectly understand or control.

BE PROACTIVE MOVING THROUGH GRIEF

NOBODY LIKES TO BE UNCOMFORTABLE—LET'S JUST face it. Grief and loss are hard, and they're also part of life. Understanding that both of these things can be (and are) true at once makes it extra important to shore up your foundation of support early and often. While you can't control what happens to you, you can control whether or not you have a structure in place to deal with the hard times. As you surround yourself with colleagues, friends, and mentors, choose ones who you can both celebrate with and who will be there for you not only in fair weather. Building this foundation is far easier to do before tragedy strikes than after, and it makes it less likely that you'll become stuck in your grief.

I've watched my mom in particular evolve through different stages of grief. She seems to be reaching the point where she understands what makes her happy. Sometimes, I help her revisit the highlights of her week to feel better: making dinner plans with a friend, visiting her granddaughters, seeing a movie with another friend, going to an event at church, and so on. When she gets out of the house, she feels better.

In the midst of grief and depression, it can be hard for people to see those bright spots. I tend to power through, but I've had to learn not everyone operates the same way I do. When you find yourself going through something tough, I encourage you to be honest with yourself and focus on what you can proactively do to make yourself feel better— one minute at a time, one day at a time. It adds up.

THE SYRUP

● There will always be uncertainty in your life, but if you have the right foundation, the right mentors, and the right tribe, they can lift you up when you feel like you don't have anything to give.

● Significant growth can come through trials if you're willing to sit with the lessons under the surface. You can become a stronger person, and then you can help somebody else. I'm a hospice volunteer now, which was not a part of my life ten years ago. Back then, I couldn't imagine that work. It sounded so depressing. I've found it's not, though. I learned about myself and what's meaningful through tragedy and struggle.

● Sometimes, in the middle of stress, you'll have blinders on. Surviving feels all-consuming. It's important to remember the way things are now is not how they'll always be. Remembering that fact can help give you the strength to push through instead of becoming paralyzed.

● No matter what comes your way—bad or good—nothing is forever. Everything passes. So, appreciate the good while you have it and cultivate being fully present. Don't despair when the bad happens. Guess what. That will change too.

● Be slow to say yes. If you become too busy and stressed out, it's hard to see how much you've overcommitted and regain your balance. It's important to take the time to process what you're saying yes to, or you can end up having nothing for yourself at the end of the day.

● Find your balance among humility, accomplishments, and knowing yourself and your strengths.

● Use your creativity and resourcefulness to seek satisfaction in different areas of your life. Sometimes, people get complacent and just keep going through the motions without stopping to ask what truly makes them happy or what they could add or change to make their life better.

Part Two

LOVE

FIND THE RIGHT FIT

MY HUSBAND AND I HAVE BEEN TOGETHER FOR SEVenteen years now. I got that man to tell me he loved me after two weeks. He was engaged previously when he was younger, in his twenties. He was in love, but at the end of the day, he realized it wasn't a fit.

After he and I had been together for about a year, he said, "You know, I love you, but I also like you." He also said he thought that was more important in some ways. Young people, and young women in particular, can fall in love with being in love and want everything to be perfect, like a rom-com. Love is certainly important, sure. But it takes more than that.

I was married before Sean. In that relationship, I didn't have the mushy love feelings, but I thought I could cultivate them. Why? Simple: he was stable, I loved the idea of love, and I talked myself into it.

Not surprisingly, that marriage ended. I wasn't with the right guy, but now I am. It can be tempting to settle for whoever's near us, but we change so much from our early- to mid-twenties. In my first marriage, I tried to like everything my husband liked, until I became so resentful that I couldn't stand it. When we got together, I didn't even know who I was as a person enough to follow my own passions and think about whether we were truly compatible.

When Sean and I got married, I was thirty-two, and we'd been together for almost seven years. We had such a good foundation that it feels like hanging out with a friend. We can be solid and ourselves, without settling. I'm also madly in love with him, and he's definitely my soulmate. Our relationship is sustainable and true.

People advise marrying your best friend, which I have mixed feelings about since it's not realistic to make one person your everything. At the same time, you do need to *like* the person. There are days I'm a mess, and my husband still likes me—and vice versa. That matters.

BELIEVE IN LOVE, EVEN IF IT'S AT THIRD SIGHT

I THINK THE MOST CHANGE FOR WOMEN HAPPENS between the ages of twenty-three and twenty-six. I've told all my little cousins they aren't allowed to get married until after they're twenty-six. Most of us graduate from college around the time we're twenty-two. It's common for our parents to have to bail us out or help us cosign on an apartment. By twenty-six, you're on your own. I was twenty-six when I started my company. I know people in their forties and fifties who are still on their parents' "payroll," but by my mid-twenties, I was making money, living my own life how I wanted to live it, and didn't need my parents to bail me out.

I was married when I met Sean at a Manhattan Chamber of

Commerce networking event at Connolly's Pub. We were talking about what we did for a living, our businesses, referral sources, and so on. I thought he was good looking but didn't really give him a second thought. Then we ran into each other again a month later and decided to get together for breakfast, which is a very New York way to connect one-on-one in business. We talked for two hours, and I left thinking about how I could get a guy like him but instead had an unemployed husband living off of me.

I started to remember my worth, and I saw I'd settled tremendously. My first husband was not a bad guy, but I got my head on straight about my life during that marriage.

I wasn't a cheater, so I wasn't going to have an affair. I put together a happy hour with some friends and told them to consider Sean the "licked cookie"—code for *don't try to date him, but let me know what you think.* Everyone loved him. Afterward, I went to a rooftop bar with my friends, Carmen and Cara, and Cara's partner called. She told him she couldn't talk because "Susan's either going to have an affair or leave her husband."

Hearing her say those words, I realized she was right. I was done. That night, my then-husband picked me up from the train station, and I told him I wanted a divorce. I knew if I was having such strong feelings for someone else, then I wasn't in the right relationship. Also, Sean was on my laminated list. I'd talked myself into a third of what I wanted, and it wasn't enough.

I wouldn't necessarily recommend doing what I did, but I do recommend the aspect of going with your gut. People talk about love at first sight, which wasn't quite what happened, but it was love at third sight.

After that two-hour breakfast, he knew my life's story and knew what he was getting into. After I left my husband, we went to a concert together in Long Island. Sean was an eligible bachelor who had some "irons in the fire," so to speak, and I asked him what we were going to do. I was walking away from a marriage, so if he wasn't in, I couldn't be strung along. He saw he could like me and love me, and he committed. That wouldn't have been possible for either of us if we weren't honest about what we deserved and the fit we were each looking for.

CONNECTING EMOTIONALLY

WHEN I MET SEAN, MOST PEOPLE AT THE TIME DIDN'T know I was married because my ex and I had eloped. Even my family didn't know I was married until I was getting out of that relationship—which I also don't recommend. The Reader's Digest version of the story is that I'd gotten married for taxes and health insurance. I'd literally called my CPA and said, "Yeah, we love each other. But is it better to get married before or after the new year?" Because my ex-husband was unemployed and we had the income differential, it was better to get married before. Like a lot about that relationship, it was calculated and transactional. (If you want the unabridged version of the story, you'll have to buy me a cup of coffee.)

I sometimes handle my personal life like I do my business: with pros, cons, worst-case scenarios, and financial considerations. The problem is if everything is business, you can miss out on the emotional piece. With Sean, I allowed myself to be emotional and vulnerable. By the time we got together, I was healthier physically and mentally, which laid a better foundation than I was capable of having with my "starter" husband.

Sean and I were together for several years, but our engagement was short—just six months. I honestly never thought we'd get married because Sean wasn't a big believer in marriage. We had a domestic partnership certificate from New York and living wills—the works.

Sean is from Philadelphia, and that year, his beloved Phillies were in the final playoffs to head into the World Series. They lost. I'd tried to stay up with him for the games, but I fell asleep for that last one. He was coming to bed, and I asked him, half-asleep, if they'd won. I hugged him and said I was sorry—not because I especially cared about the game (I'm a Royals fan after all), but I cared about how much *he* cared about it. I barely even remember that interaction because I was only half awake, but he said right then he knew I was everything he could ask for. He knew marriage was the one thing I wanted, so a week later, he proposed to me, just before his fortieth birthday.

When he proposed to me, we'd already planned on going to Costa Rica for Christmas. He loves Las Vegas, but my "girl logic" was: "the only way we're going to Vegas is if we're getting married." That was my hard line.

When he asked, we were sitting next to each other on the couch watching *Blue Bloods*.

"Hey, I've been thinking about Costa Rica," he said. I said, "I know I need to put a deposit down, but we just shucked out a lot of money for your party, so give me a couple of weeks."

Without missing a beat, he said, "I know, but considering how upset your mother is going to be if we aren't there for Christmas and what your dad said to me this morning, I think we should get our parents together and go to Vegas instead."

I did a triple take.

"Are you asking me to marry you?" I screeched. "Are you absolutely sure?" (There may have been a couple f-bombs thrown in there for good measure.)

"Yes," he said. "I don't have a ring for you yet because I want you to have exactly what you want, so we'll design it together." (Fun fact: since then, I've helped three friends design engagement rings.)

Since this was something I honestly didn't know was in

the cards for us, I remember saying, "I'm going to call my mom, and once I do, there are no takebacks. So, if you need a takeback, now is the time." He smiled. If you know Sean, Sean doesn't do anything Sean doesn't want to do, so he had thought it through, and he was certain. Needless to say, there were no takebacks, and I gave him an obvious *YES*. We called our families. We got his dad on the phone, and his dad said the greatest day of his life was when the doctor put Sean in his arms, and our engagement was the second-greatest day of his life. We laugh about that comment now because that means the second-greatest day wasn't Sean's brother being born or his dad's own marriage to his wife Cathy.

Our wedding rings are engraved on the inside. His says, "No takebacks," and mine says, "Vegas." His birthday doubled as an engagement party in November, and then we got married the following May.

Having this level of emotional connection is possible and beautiful, and I wish it for everyone, especially you.

"EVERY TRASH CAN HAS A LID."

MY MOTHER-IN-LAW, CAROL, FREQUENTLY SAYS THAT every trash can has a lid, meaning there's someone for everyone. In fact, I think there are multiple people out there for you, not just one soulmate. My husband always talks about how all women can be moody and all guys can be jerks, so you just need to match up with the right person for your jerkiness and moodiness.

When I was younger, I laminated a list of what I wanted to find in a relationship: telling me he loves me, loving his family, bringing me flowers "just because"—all aspects that spoke to the character of the man I wanted to be with. I kept that list in my wallet for years to remind myself I deserved all those qualities and that the person I imagined wasn't too good to be true.

I have friends who get into relationships and are crying after a month. If you're crying after a month, how do you think it will be a year from now? My mother-in-law also says, "As good as it is today is as good as it's going to be." That attitude is a little cynical, I admit, but there's a piece about it that I like. Be honest with yourself to see if you're just settling and going through the motions, so you're not alone. Don't you deserve to be in real love in a truly healthy relationship?

Experts always talk about how much work relationships are, but when you're with the right person, I don't think it's that hard. Communication is key. Sean and I have only had about three fights in our whole relationship because we talk directly and move on.

Of course, there are things that annoy him about me, and vice versa. (Just ask him how much he loves it when I load the dishwasher.) One of our inside jokes is "Where's the umbrella, Susan?" He once asked me that question while looking at a closed closet door, and I said, "Maybe you should open the door and see instead of asking me." Ten years later, I found him a Valentine with a man looking at a refrigerator full of butter on plates and asking his wife, "Where's the butter, honey?" It's good to laugh at yourself and have a sense of humor about your missteps and shortcomings.

It's also important to know each other, and Sean knows me. He knows what I've gone through with my family and in life. He understands I need time to process my thoughts internally before I come to him to talk through ideas. We also know our roles in the relationship. I *try to remember* to ask him what he wants before I give advice. Active listening is different from passive listening, and I don't want to jump in as a fixer when he doesn't want to be rescued. (The same skill is important with friends and other relationships too, by the way.)

I found my lid, and he found his. And it feels damn good.

KNOW YOUR WORTH

THE LAMINATED LIST OF QUALITIES I WANTED IN A partner reminded me of my worth and was a visual representation of what I wanted. Checking my fixer tendencies is about knowing myself—something we discussed in Part I: "Self," but that's important in a different context when it comes to love.

When Sean and I got together, my mom said I was kind of harsh with him. She thought I was too direct and forceful, but I told her I'd learned from my first marriage. I was never going to let him come back to me and say he didn't know how I felt about a situation.

For instance, we don't have children and don't plan to have children. We had that conversation early in our relationship because that issue is a dealbreaker. We also have largely separate finances. In my first marriage, we commingled all our accounts. I learned never to do that again. If you go through a divorce, you learn about those boundaries. Sean and I each have our own money and then split joint expenses fifty-fifty by funding an "operating account." That way, we don't need each other's permission to buy and do what we want.

Sean was always concerned that people stop trying in marriages because they get complacent and take each other for granted. My parents set a great example for me on that front because even though they had kids, they still had date nights and made time for each other. Today, kids tend to be everything to a family, whereas in previous generations, the spouse came first, and the kids fell in line, which I think allows adults to have their own identity. If everything's for your kids, you aren't actually modeling for them the importance of selecting the proper spouse or life partner.

My mom and dad went through premarital counseling required by the church, and the minister said they had to learn to love each other even when they're being unlovable. People talk about marriages being fifty-fifty, but they're not. Someone always picks up the slack, and the division shifts over time. There just needs to be an ebb and flow, and people need to define their roles. For instance, Sean is better at finance, so he handles that aspect, even though I could myself. I used to do most of the cooking, but then I got too busy, and now he chips in more. I appreciate that we can expand outside those traditional gender roles. In our marriage, I'm not allowed to load the dishwasher because he says I can't do it right. We've figured out the division of labor that works for us.

These things work for us. They might not work for you, but the point is bigger than checking accounts or chores or other day-to-day arrangements: we keep our own identities within our relationship instead of losing ourselves.

"YOU NEVER REGRET THE TIME YOU SPEND."

MY FRIEND JOEY PASSED AWAY IN JANUARY 2021. I'D been friends with him for twelve or thirteen years. He was larger than life. You'd picture him being on a barstool at Bada Bing, like in *The Sopranos*. He was half-Irish and half-Italian and had some ties to some crooked noses. He was very plainspoken and had a third-grade education, but he was brilliant. He had a laugh like the male version of Fran Drescher that created so much joy.

He'd had a massive heart attack, a stroke, and a quadruple bypass. He was never expected to speak again, let alone walk. Still, he worked hard through rehabilitation. He walked with a pronounced limp, but he was able to function and have a very successful career. He was one of those guys with a rough exterior and was an impeccable dresser during his working years when he'd wear magnificent suits.

He never shied away from giving zingers. He was super direct and wouldn't hesitate to slam you.

When I started out in insurance in New York, I also worked as a personal trainer because I couldn't survive on $24,000 a year in the city. I had a training client, Don, who was the uncle of someone from *The Sopranos*. Growing up in Missouri, I wasn't exposed to as many colorful people or even just different cultures. In the Midwest, I grew up with certain values but also stereotypes, including about Italians.

Once I was complaining to Don about something that happened at work. He asked me, "Do you want me to have a carpet delivered to him?" I didn't understand what he meant. Why would I want a gift delivered to someone who was pissing me off? He explained that in old mob times, "delivering a carpet" was to roll the person up in it after they had been whacked.

I told Joey that story, and he thought it was hilarious. Of course, he knew all about those times without me having to explain.

My dad was diagnosed with cancer in 2008, and I'd started my company in June 2005. I told Joey I was stressed out. I knew I needed to show up for my family, but I also had an incredible amount of responsibility with my work. I was handling all aspects of the business with just one part-time worker.

Joey listened to my struggle, and he told me, "You'll never regret the time you spend with your dad." He reminded me that people always talk about wishing that they had more time with family, but they never say they wish they could take that time back and work more. I took that advice to heart, and for the next ten years, I made my dad a priority. I went home and visited my parents at least four times a year—and even more frequently during the year before my dad died.

I moved back for most of the summer of 2018, before he passed. Sometimes you don't realize how much a piece of advice impacts your life until after the fact, and that was certainly the case with Joey's guidance. He reached me at a time when I was feeling overwhelmed and helped me see the forest for the trees. I'm grateful for that clarity.

It's hard to know the best choice in advance, but I benefited from setting up my company for remote work from the very beginning. I didn't realize what a blessing that was until I needed to travel all over the country for work and be present to help care for my father.

When Joey passed away, I helped put together his memorial service, which was on Zoom because of Covid. I asked various people in his life for their favorite memory, quote, or story from their time with him as well as pictures. There were so many nuggets of good information that he'd passed along to people, and I shared them during the service. His wife said she printed out the PowerPoint from the event and treasures it because it truly captured his essence.

I'm someone who gets things done, so it's common for me to get tapped to take care of logistics like planning a service. In this case in particular, I feel like I gained so much in the process. I got to know him better and receive or revisit so much of his advice. I'm grateful to him because I have no regrets about my relationship with my father. I know I was a good daughter. Without Joey's advice, maybe I wouldn't have shown up, and I would have had more to grapple with in my grief as a result. I feel blessed to have known him and learned from him when I did.

Joey was such a giver, from fostering the relationships in his life to helping animals. He always had a couch to crash on or five dollars to hand out to someone going through a hard time. The fall before he passed away, my friend Kat and I met up with him for coffee in the park across the street from my office on 5th Avenue. He was right; I'll never regret the time I spent with him, either. We knew he had health problems but still didn't expect him to pass away at fifty-nine years old, so I'm grateful we found ways to connect, even through Covid, instead of waiting.

My father's death brought with it a great amount of clarity for me, and so did Joey's. I think women in particular have a hard time saying no. We feel pressure to say yes to everyone and be people pleasers. However, "no" is a complete sentence. I've learned to spend time on what I *want* to spend time on now. I spend my time with people who make a difference in my life and whose relationships mean the most to me. Life is short, and you can spread yourself too thin if you're not careful. Then, when events arise that really matter, you might not have the bandwidth for them. Thinking about investing in relationships and never regretting that time offers an important perspective.

Joey lived by his own advice, since he was on borrowed time after his stroke. He became a servant leader and gave of himself because he knew the value of connection with other people. He was the definition of love in action.

A BIG PART OF LOVE IS JUST... SHOWING UP

MY DAD WAS A STRONG, ACCOMPLISHED PERSON, SO IT was hard to watch his physical decline and see him in those moments of low oxygen. He played football in school. He maintained his fitness throughout his military career and afterward. He was always doing pushups and walking on the treadmill. He grew up on a dairy farm that is still in our family, and it includes timber. He'd go and cut wood and find serenity in nature. It was hard to watch him lose those abilities and lose so much weight. His speech was also drastically impacted after his final surgery about a year before he passed, so we had to pay attention to understand him.

People would want to visit him, and we had to pick our times to anticipate how he'd feel. One of the greatest last visits he had was with a man named Ed Manring, who was the judge after my father in their county. They'd both also been prosecuting attorneys (you remember the Mr. Manring who was the prosecuting attorney I had to get the number for when I hit Darryl's truck? He's one and the same!) and members of the same fraternity. He'd told me he wanted to visit, but I warned him I'd be in there to interpret his speech. Ed showed up with flashcards that said, "Yes," "No," "Maybe," and "Bullshit."

When my dad's mind was active, his oxygen levels stayed up even when he wasn't on the machine. He didn't have the oxygen on while Ed was visiting, but they had a great conversation. Ed told him about cases going on in the county and reminisced about my dad's old cases. After Ed left, I checked my dad's oxygen, and it was at 97 percent, even though he hadn't been on the tank for over an hour. I actually called Ed afterward to tell him how huge that visit was. This is proof to me that the deepest of friendships have roots in something so strong it can only be described as platonic love.

Ed has become a mentor of mine since my dad passed. Since I can no longer talk over my expert witness work with my dad or get his pep talks, Ed has taken on that role. Before a deposition, I'll text or call to see if he has any advice. People talk about how it takes a village to raise a child. I'm in my early forties and don't need to be raised anymore, but it's been so wonderful to have some of my dad's friends embrace me in a fatherly way in his absence.

I still ask for advice and am still learning. I know I haven't reached some destination where I no longer need mentorship. Without my father, it's a gift to have other mentors step up and support me. We all go through different seasons of life when we need help. None of us can handle everything, even if we sometimes think we can make it on our own. At the end of the day, it's powerful to have a sounding board and people in your corner. I don't think Ed or I ever specifically sought out the relationship we have, but he saw the need and cared about my dad, so he cares about me too. I was open to him taking on that role.

Ed's visit also stands out to me because he didn't treat my dad like a patient or a dying man. He treated him with deep respect and love, and I'm forever grateful.

RESPECT DIFFERENCES

YOU BRING YOUR PAST AND EXPERIENCES TO DIFFER-ent relationships. This is just a fact. My mom grew up with a father who never haggled because that's who he was. By contrast, my father grew up with some of the best bargain-ers in the state of Missouri. He never paid full price, and he'd always loved to wheel and deal.

My mom talked about buying their first house in Columbia, a little modest brick house at 907 Hope Place in Columbia, Missouri. It was listed for $20,000 in the early seventies, and my dad prepped my mom that they'd try to give a sob story about just getting out of active duty and being a poor student. He told her just to look pitiful. They got there, my dad offered $17,500, and my mom actually gasped. He told her to go wait in the car. They grew up in very different situations. My father went to a one-room schoolhouse in

Gentry County in kindergarten and first grade and traveled by pony cart. He was born on the farm, whereas my mom was a city girl who grew up outside of Chicago.

Watching their differences taught me to remember people come from different circumstances and have their own pasts, and it's important to be willing to understand their perspective.

I grew up in a family where people asked why you would hire someone to do something you could do yourself, whereas my husband grew up in a family that asked why you would do something yourself if you could hire someone. After being together for seventeen years, we know our differences and lean into them rather than letting them become obstacles. They make us better individually and better together.

REMEMBER—WE'RE ALL HUMAN

SOMETIMES WE PUT OUR RELATIONSHIPS ON SUCH A pedestal that there's no place to go but down. This dynamic can happen with parents, siblings, spouses, and friends. We don't mean to sabotage the connection in that way, but we do, and it's not fair. The first time someone does something imperfect, it can feel shattering.

Remember everyone is human, even your spouse or your parents. Keep your expectations in check to avoid animosity, regret, and disappointment. Sean is amazing, but he isn't perfect. He doesn't have to be perfect to be perfect for me. My dad was amazing, but he wasn't perfect. He didn't need to be perfect to be perfect for me.

THE SYRUP

● You'll never regret spending quality time with those you love. If you get hit by a bus tomorrow, you want people to remember you for how you connected with them.

● Spending time is more than being physically there. Remember to *listen*. People tend to spend so much of conversations thinking about the next thing they want to say, but really hearing someone else is a deeper skill. After being inducted into "The Dead Dad's Club," I became a better listener, and I encourage people to say what they mean instead of being guarded or holding themselves back.

● Be open to taking on a supportive role to other people. Be open to being a mentor when you're ready. At the same time, accept help when you need it. Those relationships evolve organically when you leave room for them.

- My dad's death hurt so much because we loved so much. The alternative is so much worse: to be complacent and indifferent. After losing him, I started telling people I loved them more often and more freely, both among my family and my friends. I say what I mean and how I feel because I might not have the chance again.

- My husband and I have been married for seventeen years, and we've had maybe three fights because we're healthy communicators. He often says men will not volunteer for manual labor, but they'll do it if asked. In other words, make the request. Don't be afraid to ask for help, even though it's hard, because you can't expect people to read your mind.

- If people are bringing you down, it's okay to take personal inventory and see whether you have outgrown certain people in your life. When I left my first husband, I changed—he didn't. He was the same man I married, which is fine. He was a good guy, but he wasn't my guy for the long term. Realizing that truth wasn't a failure. When I hear someone's getting divorced, I congratulate them. It wasn't working for a reason, and moving on is the first step to happiness.

Part Three

FAMILY

LET THE JOY SHINE THROUGH

MY DAD AND I WERE TWO PEAS IN A POD. WHEN I WAS a kid, he always said I had my head in the game. We'd be working on a project, and he'd ask me to get a hammer, but I'd already have it ready for him in my hand. We had similar thought processes. We could accomplish more in a ten-minute conversation together than most people can accomplish in three days.

I often serve as an expert witness now. Because Dad was a judge, he had great joy and pride in my working on legal cases. I'd call and talk through issues with him to get his advice before a deposition or trial, so I could benefit from a judge's point of view. Don't get me wrong: I can be a talker. (I am my mother's daughter, after all.) But for the most part, my dad and I would say, "Give me the Reader's Digest version" of the story and cut right to what we needed to know. When it was he and I together, we got right to the point.

I know I was a good daughter. I showed up. I don't have regrets about my relationship with my father, and I feel fortunate in that. I know I'm lucky because I have friends who struggle with their relationships with their adult children to this day. If something happened, they'd have unresolved feelings to deal with. I was always my dad's buddy. We did projects together in the garage and on the farm. I'd work in the garden with him. That closeness never subsided.

Before we engaged hospice, we had hard, gut-wrenching, emotional conversations. Something that had always been so near to my dad's heart was our farm. Even though he was a Major General in the Air Force and a Circuit Court Judge in his civilian life, he was a farm boy first. That's why it was a priority of his to have conversations with me around how it all worked. One afternoon, he had me invite Larry Slayden over—a man who had done sharecropping with my dad for years. It was important for my dad to pass the baton to me, so to speak, to be able to have conversations with Larry. After my "Farming 101" class, I walked Larry out, and he told me I needed to take my dad out to the farm.

"It's in your dad's soul. It's a big part of who he is and where he finds joy," Larry reminded me. I walked right back in the house and told Dad we should go.

"We don't have to," he replied.

"Well, where else do you have to be?"

He smiled, and we walked out to the pickup truck. We drove the entire property, him at the wheel. He talked to me about the farm and the land under CRP, which is a restoration program. He explained how we got a bonus because he planted wildflowers for butterflies and other pollinators. We were about to go, and he asked me to wait a minute because he said he couldn't come to the farm and not pee outside. He said he was having so much fun and that I always appreciated the farm more than anyone else in the family. I'm not so sure that it's true, but I know that it was important to my dad. I've made it a priority even though I live in NYC.

That drive is one of my last really good memories of my dad. I treasure my childhood and my adult life with him. We were always kindred spirits. We were the ones who herded cats to get the rest of the family to go places. We'd tell them we had to be someplace half an hour earlier just to arrive on time. We were partners in that role; I don't think I completely realized this until the night of his visitation. I was trying to get everyone out the door to be on time. I remember looking up, almost like a prayer to my dad, and saying "Dad, I need some help here." Miraculously, everyone came together and got where they needed to be on time...ish.

My brother Matt and my mother are wonderful, and I could write entire books about their impact on me too. But there was only one Roger Combs. It's hard to continue on without him, but I'm also glad I have so many great memories to draw from. When I'm struggling, I remember his advice to me and the quotes I've gathered. I dig under the grief and let the joy shine through.

A CANARY AND A COLOR TV

MY MOM GREW UP OUTSIDE CHICAGO AND THEN GRAD-uated from high school in the Washington, DC metro area. One of the first places she worked was American Airlines. Then, she worked for Amtrak when it was called Auto Train, supervising the route from DC down to Florida. She met my dad in DC when he was a helicopter pilot in the Marine Corps and had just come back from Vietnam. They met at a singles bar in the city. My dad asked for my mom's number, but he was in the Marine Corps and newly divorced with a four-year-old child (my brother David). She had some hesitation, so she told him he could call American Airlines and ask for Gloria.

A month passed, and then they ran into each other at the same bar. He said, "Sally, right?" She said, no, her name was Gloria. He said no wonder she'd never called him back—

when he called the airline, he'd asked for Sally. My mother repeated this story for years until—ten years after they'd been married—my dad finally admitted he'd never called and had actually known her name was Gloria. He was just being smooth, and six months after that second meeting, they were married (which was more common in 1972).

My mom was a big city girl and loved Washington, DC. My grandfather was a paratrooper in the Army, and then he was a superintendent of schools before he went onto work for the Department of the Navy as an education specialist, so my mom went to about eight different schools in her lifetime. As a result, she was adamant about not being a military wife because she didn't want to put kids through that experience. My dad decided if he wasn't going to stay active-duty military, he wanted to go back to Missouri and attend law school at the University of Missouri, where he already had one semester under his belt before joining the Marine Corps. They moved to Columbia, and my dad was in law school while my mom started working for a travel agency.

Many of us who have gone through a journey have had a period of having to do without. When my mom moved to Missouri, she had two prized possessions: a canary and a color TV. Well, the color TV broke on the move from DC to Missouri, and they couldn't afford to get it out of the repair shop. They made do with an old black-and-white with rabbit ears that only got fuzzy Channel 2. My dad was studying in law school, and he'd take the doorknob off the door, so my mom would leave him alone. The only thing she had to do was watch wrestling, so she got into watching it on Friday and Saturday nights.

My mother also had a green thumb, so she had various houseplants. One day, she took the prized canary out to the sun porch, so she could take care of the plants. She heard a *tweeeeet*, and the bird succumbed to heatstroke. All she valued from DC was gone, including the big city life.

My parents also talked about how their refrigerator died, and they couldn't afford to repair it, so they started going out to buy milk every morning and putting it in a styrofoam cooler. They did without for a few months until they could save up for the repair. Their dining table was a picnic set that my dad spray-painted black to make it look more elegant, and my mom ripped countless pairs of pantyhose on the rough wood of the table.

In other words, they had moxie. I've drawn from those stories during hard times of my life, like when I started selling insurance and was making only $24,000 a year. The firm deducted my health insurance, and I had $1,200 in rent, a $63–subway pass, and a cellphone. That left me with about $150 at the end of the month. It was hard, but during that time in my life, I also developed tenacity. I had the drive, desire, and perseverance I learned from my parents. I'd seen how much they'd gone through to make things work.

When my dad graduated from law school, they moved to St. Joseph, Missouri, and my dad took a job as a workers comp attorney. The whole time he stayed in reserve status in the military, in the Army National Guard, to have some extra income coming in. He changed over to the Air National Guard and eventually became the director of intel for a C-130 base in Missouri followed by a role as the Assistant Adjutant General in the State of Missouri before rising to the rank of General and heading back to DC to work.

When my father retired from the military, he had served for thirty-nine years and four months, which included a career in three branches of our armed services. My mom joked that he'd put one over on her because when they'd started getting serious, she'd put her foot down about not being a military wife. In the end, he had two full-time careers for basically my entire life. When they moved to St. Joe, she said she could handle it but didn't want to go anywhere smaller.

A few months later, though, my dad found out about a prosecuting attorney position in Gentry County, which would mean moving to King City. She agreed but said if they went any smaller, she would leave him because it only had a population of 986.

The rest of that love story is history.

DON'T FORCE FAMILY

AFTER I MOVED TO NEW YORK IN 2001, I CAME BACK for Christmas and was together with Matt and David, my brothers. Matt pointed out how very different the three of us are—our personalities, our interests, our paths, our social circles. He said, "If we weren't born siblings, we'd never be friends."

He was right. He didn't mean it in a derogatory way but rather as a way of embracing our differences.

When you notice those differences from your family, it can give you the approval you need to be yourself. Youngest children in particular sometimes get defined by their older siblings, but as the youngest, I was charting my own path at that point in a way very different from everyone around me.

Sometimes people think that their relationships with family should mirror a Hallmark movie, but those movies aren't real life. It's important to have realistic expectations and let people truly be themselves instead of trying to force them into our cookie-cutter idea of how, for instance, families relate to each other. Siblings don't have to be best friends; some are, but it's not required. Realism helps take some of the pressure off. You can have points of overlap in your relationships and also areas where you do your own thing.

My business partner is one of three girls, and she says she has a similar experience with her sisters. They'll always be close, but they're also very different people, from their interests to their professions to their musical tastes.

Matt's statement came from a loving place. There's power in having strong bonds with family, no matter how different the members might be. By embracing differences, my brother Matt and I are tremendously close. We have an almost secret language. It's not fair playing Catchphrase against us because we can communicate so well, a relationship forged by our good, shared childhood together. We understand our differences and what we're both good at. Especially in the three years since our dad has passed, Matt comes to me for the kind of advice my dad would have given because he knows I think in a similar way. I've also come to rely on Matt to be my sounding board when life happens and I need to tap out.

I'm very fortunate to have such a great family. We have conflicts sometimes, but we all love each other. I know other people who don't have that closeness and foundation to draw from. Whatever your situation, I encourage you to value the good parts but not try to force the square peg into a round hole in the areas where you diverge.

BE A GRACIOUS RECEIVER

MY BROTHER MATT GOT SICK IN THE SUMMER OF 1989. We'd gone on a big family trip to Colorado in our RV, along with my aunt, uncle, and cousin. We towed a trailer behind it. Matt had been very tired on that trip. When we came back, I had to get a physical for sports, so my parents decided to get him tested for mono or other issues at the same time. His hemoglobin and blood tests came back wonky, so they did a bone marrow tap.

After that, it was a whirlwind: the tests showed it was leukemia. My dad used his connections and called all the doctors he knew, asking them where they would go if it were their child who was sick. My parents ended up opting for St. Jude Children's Research Hospital. After the test, they all left for Memphis just a couple of days later. For the next two to three years, they lived there on and off, without me.

During that time, I stayed with my grandmother a lot as well as with my Aunt Karen and Uncle Larry from time to time. I was ten at the time of his diagnosis, and my identity effectively became the "person whose brother had cancer."

Matt was diagnosed with acute lymphoblastic leukemia (ALL). Back then, they advised not making plans beyond ten years because childhood cancer was a death sentence. They'd made strides, but he ended up going into remission and then relapsing again. At that point, he needed a bone marrow transplant and had a 16 percent chance of survival, which no one told him until later.

I had two very different parents. My dad tended to be pragmatic, and I don't think he assumed Matt would make it. My mother, on the other hand, has always said she knew God would provide and he would make it. The difference made for an interesting dynamic in the family.

Today, there's more awareness when kids get sick or encounter other tragedies because of social media. Back then, people didn't even have cell phones unless they were in specialized jobs. That meant Matt was the first kid most people in our community knew who had cancer. People held a bone marrow transplant drive to try to find a match for him. I should have been the closest match, but I didn't match, nor did anyone we knew—so we had to expand the search worldwide.

Matt prayed because he needed a sign. The next day, my dad told us they'd found twenty possible matches. His match ended up coming from Toulouse, France (even though we're not French, that I know of).

My brother is the first male bone marrow transplant performed at St. Jude Children's Research Hospital. The procedure took place thirty years ago at the time of this writing, on June 19th. When we hit the five-year mark for his transplant, that was a huge milestone. They'll never say you're cured for liability purposes, but your chances are much better if you stay in remission that long.

My dad had us stay at the Peabody Hotel to celebrate, and there was a write-up in the St. Joseph News Press. A few weeks after the article came out, Matt got a letter from a priest who read the article. He said he was blown away by the story and went on to explain that the only relics of Saint Jude outside the Holy Land are in Toulouse. He also said that, in Eastern Orthodox religions, the Feast of Saint Jude is held on June 19th—Matt's transplant day.

Then, decades later, my niece—Josephine Toulouse—was born on, you guessed it, June 19th.

But there are parts in between the bookends of that story that are important too. For example, my parents had always been the ones to help others. If someone had a death in the family, someone needed mentorship, or whatever the case might be, they were great about checking on people. We had elderly neighbors, and my family became their caretakers. When they moved into the nursing home, my dad would go by and see them almost every day. He didn't have to, as we had no blood ties to them, but it was just the right thing to do.

All through the time my family was away for Matt's treatments, people wanted to help us. My mom's close friend Lorie came over and fixed my hair for picture day. People brought food over. Families would invite me if they were taking their kids to the movies. My mom struggled with not wanting to accept so much help. She talked to the chaplain, Brent Powell, at St. Jude, who has been there since 1987, and he told her she had to be a gracious receiver. I've always remembered that lesson. People want to do things for you. Let them.

I got the advice as a kid, but then I had to give it back to my parents when they got older. When my father passed, people wanted to help but weren't sure how. My mom didn't want to be a burden on anyone, but people wanted to take her to appointments or show up in whatever way she needed. I had to remind her to be a gracious receiver and accept help.

You may need to remind yourself of that once in a while too.

FIND FAMILY TO LEAN ON

MY GRANDMA RUBY FERN WAS LIKE THE MOST PERFECT dessert; you always wanted more. She had an innate ability to make everybody feel like they were her favorite. I don't think we all realized that quality until she passed away. She had made every single one of us grandkids feel special, and we were lucky to have had good one-on-one time with her.

Hearing my cousins after she died, I realized maybe I *wasn't* her favorite. Oh, my God.

To this day, I associate flowers with the time we spent together. In the Midwest, the seed catalogs are a big deal for kids, or at least they were to me. My birthday is May 8th, and my grandmother would let me go through the catalog and pick out flowers. We'd talk about them and what grew with the sun. Then, she'd plant the flowers on my birthday.

I'm big on traditions, and I think if you don't live around family, it's natural to feel drawn to those traditions and practices that feel special. I've been very blessed to have outdoor space in most of the places I've lived, so I've always gotten my flowers from a home improvement store to plant on the weekend of my birthday. It's a tradition that honors who my grandmother was.

Honestly, she was everyone's grandma. Her funeral was packed, and the nurses at the facility where she lived used to love to go into her room because she'd tell dirty jokes and entertain them. She was so loving. She always consoled us anytime we got frustrated with something when we were kids, or we couldn't get something figured out. Even in high school if a boy didn't ask me to the dance or something, she'd just say, "Oh, honey," and comfort me. She was always wickedly funny. I'll never forget one story: one of my cousins got married, and there was some wedding drama. When we discussed it later, she exclaimed, "We just need him to hold her down, and we'll just pull out that wild hair, and she'll come around." Needless to say, the wild hair was never found, and that marriage ended in divorce!

I spent a lot of time with her after Matt was diagnosed with cancer. During that time, my grandma took me to school, picked me up, and took care of me. She used to take blankets and lay them on the heating stove for a couple of minutes to get them nice and warm. Then, she'd lay one of them on me and tuck it all around me. She used to call me her "Papoose" since I was the darkest grandchild that favored the Combs side of the family the most (the side we were always told was part Cherokee).

In high school, I remember spending summers at her house going through some of her recipes, and she'd teach me how to make them. My grandparents were dairy farmers, and my mom always said her mother-in-law worked harder than three men. She'd be out milking and then come in and make a big spread for lunch and dinner. She worked hard because that's farm life. She could make a pie in five minutes with fresh raspberries she'd pick that grew out back in the morning. She'd make homemade cinnamon rolls and get them to rise faster by putting them on the heating stove in the corner of the kitchen. As kids, we learned so much from watching and listening to her.

At her house, I used to make a beeline for the pantry and break into the homemade strawberry preserves or brown sugar. My mom would find me around age four or five just eating them with a spoon.

I have many sweet memories of my time at her house. I remember specifically the day before my brother and my parents went to Memphis for his treatment: we got a puppy. They'd promised before the diagnosis, and my dad said the dog would give me something to take care of and focus on. After all, I was ten years old and worried about my brother.

He was right, as usual.

The dog's name was Gus. Once, we were getting ready to go to a country church in Island City where I was related to or knew everyone. I couldn't find Gus and felt so worried. This was before cell phones. My grandma called my uncle to help me look. I was running all over the place outside, since we'd only had Gus for a week. He didn't even know his name yet.

I ran outside and saw a pile of bones and grey fur, which freaked me out even more. Grandma told me they were just from a possum. I felt so low, and I was sitting on the couch wallowing in my worry, when I looked down behind the chair and saw the dog was sleeping right there.

It kind of went that way with Grandma: she was a calm place, someone to lean on, a warm blanket, the embodiment of the reassurance of the dog under the chair. She wasn't going anywhere when I needed her. If that's not love, I don't know what is.

EASY KEEPER

I HAD A ROUGH TIME WHEN MY FAMILY WAS AWAY IN Memphis with Matt for his treatments. My dad would admit that before Matt got sick, I was probably a little spoiled because I was the youngest and the girl in the family. After the diagnosis, though, that went away. I got my attention by being what my parents would call "the easy keeper," which I think presented problems for me later on. My brother got lots of attention and gifts because he was so gravely ill. I was just a kid, so I felt some jealousy. My mom talks about her regrets over leaving me behind, but I don't think I would have done well in a big city. Though I was popular and fit in with my friends in my small town, I don't think I would have fared so well back then as a roly-poly kid with a bad perm and a quick mouth in inner city Memphis.

My parents did the best they could at the time. They could reflect back later and wish they'd made some different choices, but we got into a routine. My parents took turns flying back and forth to spend time with me, Matt, and each other. My father was in the military, so he was able to work out of a base in Memphis, and then he scheduled his court cases for the days he was home. My parents put their family first, and that was important.

I always had the reputation of being "the easy keeper," even before Matt's illness. If I had an appointment, I'd ask my dad what time it was and set my own alarm, even at six or seven years old. I'd be sitting by the door fifteen minutes before we needed to pull out. Like my dad said, I always had my head in the game. People didn't have to harp on me to do my homework, practice, or get to school on time. I was responsible. Those are good qualities, but I've realized they also mean I can get overlooked sometimes.

I am the fixer of my family and stepped into the role even more after my dad died. Sometimes, I have to remind people to ask me how I'm doing or check on me. It's a common story for people to assume the person who has their shit together doesn't need any help or to be checked on. Over functioning is a coping mechanism, though, so we still need support.

Even if you're high functioning, you still have to be a gracious receiver. You can't do everything yourself. Kids have to accept help because they don't have much choice or control, and sometimes, we forget that lesson in adulthood. We don't want to bother people or intrude. I don't ask for many favors, but when I do, I remember not to feel guilty if I would gladly do the same favor for someone else.

Sometimes, I have to remind myself to ask for help and notice when I'm struggling to keep my head above water. I'm fortunate to have a good tribe to support me. I can tap people when I need to. In general, though, I handle my business and tend to be efficient in my life.

When people offer to help you, they're desperate to show you how much they care. They feel empathetic. If they're part of "The Dead Dad's Club," they want to be supportive because they know how it feels.

When you ask for help, of course you don't want to wear out your welcome, but be honest with yourself about the balance of a given relationship. Often, one person contributes more than the other. If you're not getting anything out of a relationship and feel like the other person only drains your energy, then you can either ask for more help or move on.

My closest relationships have a healthy give and take; they don't expect me to save them all the time without offering anything in return. If you tend to be a giver, be careful that you don't give so much you run out of anything for yourself.

TAKE COMFORT THAT DEEP PAIN AND DEEP LOVE ARE INTERTWINED

WHEN OUR FAMILY DECIDED TO ENGAGE HOSPICE FOR my father, he said something I'll never forget:

"It hurts so much because we've loved so much."

When this quote applies, it's a sign of a life well lived with meaningful relationships. It would be tragic if a person's death didn't hurt because it would mean their life made no difference. Loss hurts precisely because people touch the lives of others, and their presence matters. Being a good person and showing up for people means so much, and when you live that way, then things will never be the same after you're gone.

There's so much I didn't anticipate when my dad passed away and I joined "The Club." Still, I took consolation in the comfort I got from people who had walked in my shoes. Because of that experience, I learned how to offer meaningful comfort to others. Before my dad died, I'd offer my condolences to people who lost family members, but I was essentially just paying lip service because I didn't understand. I couldn't fully hear what they were going through.

My own sister-in-law, Joan, lost her father about six years before I lost my own father. I can honestly say I failed her then—not because I meant to, but just because I didn't appreciate the pain and loss she went through until I went through it myself. It was no wonder why she was a rock to our family when my dad was dying. She had experienced it firsthand. She was a member of "The Club." She had been very close to her father as well, so she knew what my brothers and I were in for.

After Dad passed and we met with the minister to plan the Missouri service, we were all emotionally exhausted. We simply couldn't think straight when he would ask us questions like, "What was special about Roger?" Though we all had countless stories, in those raw moments, we had trouble articulating them. I remember Joan smiling and saying,

"Roger made everyone feel important. When he would talk to you, he was fully present and focused on what you were saying." She was so right. And that goes to show that sometimes we need those around us to give us the words when we don't have them.

Now, when I see someone post about loss on social media, I know what they're feeling and how much their life has been impacted. I reach out to them and tell them I know it's such a shitty club that you never want to join, and I hope they'll be gentle on themselves and let people help them. Women in particular carry a heavy burden to keep families together, but sometimes they need to let others step in for them in times of grief. They need to be taken care of too. Because of my experience, I know these truths firsthand and can genuinely empathize, not just offer platitudes.

Many people helped me through my loss, including people I probably hadn't physically seen in fifteen or twenty years. They knew what I was going through, though, and stepped up. The comfort they gave me inspired me to continue that gift with people who are hurting. I also felt moved to write more personal magazine articles and speak directly to people who were in my shoes or would be in the future and say, "I see you."

There's a college friend I hadn't seen in over twenty years who I reached out to after her father passed away, and I continue to check on her from time to time. I realized from my own experience that plenty of people think of you in the moment or the couple of weeks after a death, but you're still hurting and in need of support for months. Sometimes it's almost more consoling to hear from someone six months after a loss and know people are still thinking of you. It's important to make those connections and ask people how they're doing over the long haul, as well as on milestone days like Father's Day.

Some people say the first Christmas, the first Thanksgiving, and the first Father's Day are the hardest, but they're not. The second one is when you fully realize this new reality is how your life is going to be. So, having support over the long haul means a great deal. When I see people in their first year, I know it will get worse—but at this point, I also know after that low point, you start to see glimmers of joy and hope. I can start focusing on my good memories instead of just the loss.

The bottom line? If it hurts so much because you've loved so much, you've done something right.

HAVE THE HARD CONVERSATIONS

MY FAMILY HAD TIME TO MENTALLY PREPARE FOR MY father's death. We knew what it meant when we triggered hospice, even though my mom was more Pollyannaish and said people could graduate hospice. She was technically correct, but more often than not, the process doesn't go that way.

My dad was on various medications, so he slept a lot, and I was traveling back and forth from New York. At one point, he said he was afraid he'd wake up and I'd be gone, and I wouldn't know how much I meant to him. I reminded him we could get hard, complex conversations done in five minutes that would cover what other people couldn't say in a week.

Because of my work as an expert witness in medical malpractice cases, I have a vast network of people across the United States in major hospitals. My dad wanted to go to MD Anderson for a second opinion, so I reached out to my contacts and explained the situation. I got him an appointment with the head of oncology within four days, and then I went down to Texas with him. My parents were great about never shutting me, Matt, or David out of appointments or keeping medical information a secret. If I wanted to be there and ask questions, they were fine with that, especially having gone through the experience of my brother's cancer at a young age.

This wasn't our first rodeo. Once my dad got a PET scan at MD Anderson, I started one of those hard conversations we knew how to have. I asked him if he wanted to fight. I told him not to think about us because he was the one who'd been sick for ten years. Nobody would fault him if he said he was done. He told me for himself and his family, he always wanted to try. I said that was okay with me, but if he got to the point where he was done, he just needed to tell one of us, and we'd respect that decision.

I still don't know how I had the courage to have that conversation. My palms were sweating and my voice quivered as he and I walked back from his scan, but I've learned we have the freedom to say what's in our heart, even when it's hard. Those hard conversations are the ones you *should* have. I'm so thankful we talked about his choices because then we were on the same page. We'd move forward, but he also knew it was okay to pump the brakes.

I always felt very safe around my dad. With him and with me, what you see is what you get (WYSIWYG). So, when that question was weighing on my heart, even though it was a scary topic, I knew I had to speak, or I'd have regrets. Regret is more often about the conversations we don't have than the ones we do. When we decided to trigger hospice, it was a conversation we had as a family and a decision we made together. We didn't make the decision for him, and he didn't make a proclamation; we had a conversation and reached a consensus.

I encourage you to say the things you've been wanting to say. Have the hard conversations. I was fortunate to have had conversations with my dad about his financial arrangements and his wishes for after his death, so I didn't have to guess. It's important to have clarity about what your parents' wishes are for themselves, for you, and for your siblings, or you risk getting the arrangements very wrong. Having those conversations allows you to honor their legacy. Even if you don't have a close relationship with your parents and the outcome of the conversation doesn't feel as comforting, I think directly facing the issues still leads to serenity and even simple, practical benefits. You have to deal with what they leave behind, no matter how they lived, so it's better to have the chance to say what you need to say.

There's a Stoic quote that says, "We're the children of the people we choose as parents." There are the parents we're born to, but then we also have the opportunity to surround ourselves with mentors and people who truly make a difference in our lives. If you aren't close with your parents, those people may not be related to you by blood. Regardless of the relationship, it's valuable to have insight into what they want, even if it's painful.

My husband and I set up our own trust last year because I knew what I'd dealt with helping my dad before we triggered hospice. It was extremely hard, and I don't want to be in that situation again. I know now that too much information isn't enough. There's nothing wrong with having those nitty-gritty conversations about what people want or how their wishes have changed as their marriages or life situations have changed.

RECOGNIZE YOUR ROLE

OUR MOTHER HAS STRUGGLED SINCE OUR FATHER passed, as we all have. The situation has forced us to learn our strengths and weaknesses. I know a weakness for me is navigating someone else's mental health, which is actually Matt's talent through his work as a nurse and his own experience. I can be sympathetic to those issues, but I can be too abrupt, whereas Matt truly has empathy. I tend to be a fixer, so I'm good at handling logistical problems more than being a listening ear. (My dad used to say that sometimes, with me, it was "ready, fire, aim.") As a result, Matt has been particularly supportive of our mother emotionally, while I support her in many other areas.

Differentiating our roles based on our strengths is a form of self-care too. If I give too much to too many, I have nothing left for myself, so it's good to team up with someone who thinks differently and has different skills than I do. Women in particular tend to be people-pleasers, but at the end of the day, you have to put your oxygen mask on first before helping others. Overextending yourself doesn't help in the long run.

These principles of relationships can apply to chosen family too. My friend Kris got divorced and went through a journey of self-discovery. She's very level-headed and great at giving me reality checks regarding my family. In particular, she has reminded me when I'm frustrated with my family members that they're not just my family members—they're people, independent from me, who have their own wants and needs, including love. Mothers in particular tend to lose their identity to their children, so it's important to see my mom as a woman, not just my mom.

Another role shift that often gets overlooked is the one from adult to caregiver to your family of origin. It's not uncommon to talk about the transition from child to parent, of course, but society doesn't necessarily talk about what it means to be an adult child taking over caring for family members who used to care for you.

By taking over so much for my family, I have ceased to be a child to my mother in many ways, and of course my father is gone. I miss being the kid sometimes. I coordinated my dad's military service at Arlington, which was an event with more than 200 people from six different countries. I wanted it to be perfect. During the actual funeral, though, I wailed so hard, and my mom held my hand, telling me it was okay, which allowed me to feel like a kid again.

When you're the youngest and hold all the keys to the castle, you still check in with the older siblings. Matt once told me everyone knew when I was ten years old that I was a take-charge kind of person. My role was clear.

The transition is hard and painful, but it's also an opportunity to figure out what you want your role to be now. Peer-to-peer mentoring from other people in "The Club" can help you figure out those questions. I'm not the first person to lose my dad in my thirties, so there were people I could reach out to for guidance. Even if you haven't lost a parent, depending on your family dynamics, you may need to revise your role over time. You may find yourself in more of a caretaker role and need to decide how to relate to your parents as individuals.

If you're the one who always steps up, it can be draining—because I guarantee if you're doing it in your family life, you're also doing it in your business, friendships, and elsewhere. I'm guilty of this. Some days, I envision that I'm spinning plates and praying that one doesn't fall. I bet you can relate. If you raise your hand and are a natural leader, you take on more than just the task you're volunteering to do. I tend to be the one who steps in when no one else says anything, so at this point, people look to me to take charge, which can feel heavy.

When you're climbing up, make sure you also give yourself an escape route. Don't feel guilty about needing to take a break and reset.

COVET YOUR CHOSEN FAMILY

I'VE KNOWN MY FRIEND JOHN VEON FOR OVER TWENTY years. We share Midwest values and a military connection, and I consider him family. As a former paratrooper in the 82nd Airborne with vast experience as a director for brands such as Nickelodeon and Viacom, he knows how to read people well. Once, when I was having a staffing issue and couldn't figure out how to get people on the same page, he shared some words of wisdom that I have never forgotten: "There are three kinds of people: owners, renters, and squatters. Get rid of the squatters."

Though the advice was given in a work context, it directly applies to relationships. Owners are invested wholly, renters make valid contributions but clock in and out, and squatters slide under the radar and take up space.

Though it's clear we should, sometimes in our lives, we don't want to get rid of the squatters. Women especially may be more apt to hang on when we shouldn't because we don't want to "cut someone off" or "hurt someone's feelings." But when we let go of the squatters, we open ourselves up to better and stronger relationships.

The truth is that, just like we choose our employees if we have a business or we choose our friends, we are empowered to choose our family—one made up of a mixture of owners and renters.

John is definitely an owner for me, and he's definitely a part of my chosen family. But he's not the only one.

I always had a lot of guy friends in college. That could have been because I started out in Air Force ROTC, or it could have just been my personality. After I moved to New York City, though, I quickly discovered the benefit of having strong female friends too. Two who stand out for me are Nicola, whom I met at work, and Karline, whom I met at a spa after we'd both been invited to a women in business event. (We always joke that we met naked, and it's true.) The three of us have had each other's backs since day one.

John, Nicola, and Karline are pillars in my life. I know they will always show up for me, celebrate my successes, and give me real talk when I need it. Sometimes, I think they know me better than I know myself.

These three are part of my chosen family, and we've become part of each other's real families by including each other fully in our lives. For example, I'm the godmother to Karline's two boys. To me, that's the sweet spot.

Do you have a squatter or two? It's time to consider letting them go. Who are the owners in your chosen family? If you don't know yet, it's never too late.

BRING FAMILY WITH YOU

ONE OF MY FAVORITE INSURANCE CLIENTS I'VE HAD in my career is a company that makes cool urban chandeliers out of reclaimed wood and Bunsen light bulbs: Urban Chandy. I became friends with the owner quite quickly. She always said she wanted to make me one, but I asked her to wait until I owned a home. When my husband and I bought a place over seven years ago in Queens, I finally went to her and said I was ready. I had an ask, though: my family has timber in Missouri, so I wanted to supply the reclaimed wood.

Cassidy actually met my father, and he became a wood supplier on the side sometimes. I showed my uncle Larry pictures of the chandeliers, as he was a masterful carpenter, and told him what I was dreaming the finished product would look like. I've never been a materialistic person, but

I've always been sentimental. I knew the chandelier would mean so much more to me if I could get wood from the family or the farm.

Uncle Larry and my dad got together and started finding different pieces of wood. My uncle wrote on the ends of the boards. One is from my grandparents' milk barn that burned down when I was six or seven. There's a piece from my aunt and uncle's home, which is one of the oldest wooden structures in Gentry County. There are pieces from an Osage orange tree from our timber. I also grew up across the street from a funeral home, and there's an old piece of wood from one of its coffin crates that says, "If found, put on next Batesville truck." Batesville, Kansas, is where all the coffins are typically manufactured, and that stamp is a piece of Midwestern history.

The chandelier is beautiful because it's an object that became, in a way, a chronology of my family. There are pieces of wood more than 100 years old, and my dad and my uncle participated in collecting what this client made. It has so much more meaning to me than an everyday item of home decor. It hangs over my dining room table, and it's a great conversation piece because it holds so many stories and prompts me to talk about and remember my family. It keeps them with me, always.

USE SERVICE
TO HEAL

I'VE FOUND IT'S BENEFICIAL TO REACH OUT TO OTHER people in "The Club." It heals rather than compounds grief. I became a hospice volunteer to make a living legacy to my dad and the people who supported our family through that process. Connecting with others who are grieving honors him. He was good when nobody was watching, and he taught me the value of helping others because it's right, not just to post about it on social media. Those moments happen in private. When people share their loss on social media, I connect with them privately rather than commenting publicly.

We brought in hospice about five weeks before my father died. We were fortunate to have a great long-term care policy and the ability to have hospice at home, in what my dad called his "I love me" room. It was filled with awards, accolades, and pictures from his over thirty-nine years in the military and his time as a civilian judge. They covered the walls. My mom said she never had to worry about the paint, because you couldn't see a single surface. We put the hospital bed in his "I love me" room downstairs, where he could see all the memorabilia from his career and reminders of what made him happy.

Hospice has a negative connotation among many people because they figure that's who you call a week before someone kicks the bucket. That's not the whole picture, though. The rules vary by state, but typically if someone would pass in the next six months if they did not have medical intervention, then they're eligible for whole family hospice. Our team included a chaplain, a social worker, and nurses we really liked. We were also fortunate my high school friend Kassie was the director of the hospice program. Members of the team came to my dad's memorial service because they care about the families they work with and feel like they're all in it together.

The teams support families in whatever way they're receptive to. They don't try to rub salt in the wound but rather ask how a family can make the remaining time, however long it ends up being, as comfortable as possible for the patient and are supportive of the family as well.

Before going through the experience, I never would have

known how to help people in that way or the true value of meeting people where they are, which is so much of this work. I contacted the service in New York about going through the training, and they explained they don't want people to have had a significant loss in the past year. So, I made a commitment to myself that a year after my dad passed, I wanted to be a hospice volunteer to honor him and the caregivers he and my family had during that time.

Before Covid, volunteering consisted of weekly visits with a patient whose case history you've reviewed. Maybe someone's religious, and they want you to read to them from the Bible or pray with them, for example. I had a patient who grew up in the neighborhood I live in now, which has changed a great deal. We talked about the neighborhood and what used to be on different streets. He was a Dodgers fan, and we talked about baseball. He also told me about his career as a carpenter. Giving my time in this way does as much for me as it does for the people I serve.

THE SYRUP

● Losing a parent may still be far off for you timewise. In some ways, these can be the years of calm before the storm. It's valuable to learn to take care of yourself, so you have that foundation when life hits rough patches.

● Have hard conversations with your family now. It will be difficult, but it will save confusion and grief down the road.

● Everyone grieves differently, but when you can, lean on proactive and prioritize structure in your days as you cope with the complex feelings of loss

● You can create a supportive family around you if you didn't come from one. You have the family you're born with and also the family you choose.

● Don't be afraid to ask the questions. The information you gather now could end up being priceless later on.

● You never know what someone is struggling with internally. Not all scars are visible, so be kind and try to meet people where they are.

● Never underestimate the power of removing a wild hair!

Part Four

CAREER

FIND PURPOSE IN STRUGGLE

PRIOR TO STARTING MY COMPANY, I'D BEEN WORKING for a large firm. They gave me good opportunities but not great pay. After I'd been there for a year, the CFO said the company wanted to put me in a management training program to shadow different roles and see what I liked best. I asked about the salary for the program because I was only making $24,000 a year in New York City, which doesn't go far. I was netting maybe $150 a month after rent, health insurance, and other expenses. To make ends meet, I had gotten certified as a personal trainer and was working that job on the side for additional income. I was really burning the candle at both ends. I was hopeful this management training program would offer more money. The CFO said I'd just have to "trust them."

I still don't know how the hell I did it, but I looked at him and said, "Trust doesn't pay the bills." I said I needed some concrete information if I was going to sign the agreement. He wouldn't give me a number and stood his ground: I'd have to sign the agreement or be out of a job.

I walked out.

I had a great mentor, Jim Cosares, who'd been encouraging me to start my own company before I walked away. It was scary at twenty-six years old, but he believed in me. So did my now-husband, Sean. I once sat down with Jim and made a list of pros and cons for striking out on my own. At the end of the day, the only real pro of staying with a big firm was having an office, mail services, and a business card, but he told me I could start out of my apartment, print my own cards, and go to the post office myself. Remember how we talked earlier about not knowing how a decision could impact you later on? When I walked away, all my clients came with me, and I had twice as much income coming in because I no longer had to split with the house. I had the smarts to negotiate owning my book of business from day one, which isn't really typical in my industry. That negotiation was what allowed me to create Combs & Company, LLC and not have to take any business loans or lines of credit to get it started. It was scary as hell, but in June 2021, I marked the sixteen-year anniversary of that decision.

At the time, I didn't know what I didn't know. But I knew that if I treated people well, they'd come with me. That dynamic created the foundation of my current success. My background was hospitality, so I approached the insurance business with that mindset and a service model, rather than just the transactional model. That ethos, combined with good mentorship, pushed me in the right direction.

I was able to grow something I enjoy doing and feel passionate about. I have a staff, and I make a whole lot more than $24,000 a year. I knew I could do the work on my own, but in the beginning, I had to fake it till I made it. I didn't grow up thinking I would start a business. It wasn't my dream. There's a saying about creativity—that it's what you reach for when you have no other choice. Necessity is the mother of invention.

I could have crumbled under the weight of the uncertainty, but I stood my ground. I had to roll with my circumstances, and they pushed me toward starting my own business. As an entrepreneur, you learn a tremendous amount about yourself. You grow as a person. I became so much more self-reliant and started to believe in myself. My former job forced my hand in a way, but it also allowed me to pivot to a fresh start. When it comes to your career, believe in yourself and treat people the right way, and good things will come.

SLEEP ON IT

I MET MY COLLEAGUE RUSS ABOUT TWELVE YEARS AGO when he was in corporate HR for one of the largest investment banks in the world. He grew up in El Paso, Texas, and he and his wife were both theater kids. They just celebrated thirty-seven years of marriage. They came out to New York for theater. He lived the corporate life for many years and then retired and started doing more consulting and has been able to get back to his first love: theater.

Russ is a very methodical person. He thinks through situations. He's a great guy for me to bounce a business idea off of if I have a staffing issue, such as when I'm thinking of hiring someone or letting someone go. Years ago, he said when he's in a situation and feels the desire to respond, he asks himself, "Does it need to be said, does it need to be said now, and does it need to be said by me?" Following that advice, I can't tell you how many times I've started writing a text message and then thought, *Nope, delete, delete, delete.*

Sometimes you have to let people run with scissors. Maybe they're not living their life how you would, but it's their life and their choice. My husband reminds me it's not my job to be the moral voice of reason. That tendency is one of my faults. If I encounter an outlandish statement and find myself reacting emotionally, I remember to tone check. Everyone has a phrase in their internal monologue that signals a strong reaction, whether it's "Seriously?!" or "What the fuck?" or something else. If that signal phrase pops into your head, you're about to be reactive, whether you realize it or not—you need a tone check before you get yourself in trouble.

I have a "sleep on it" folder in my email. If I feel pissed off and my eye starts twitching, I'll put the message in the folder until the next day when I have a fresh pair of eyes. If I sleep on it and still feel it needs to be said now and by me, then I will have had that distance and time to reflect before I respond so I can deliver my point appropriately. I pull in a tone checker, such as my husband or my business partner. Inevitably, they'll point out an emotion I didn't intend, which I can cut out, and recipients respond much better as a result. Often, though, the answers to Russ's questions are simply no, in which case it's good I slept on the issue and didn't react.

In emails and texts, tone, sarcasm, and other nuances are hard to convey, so you have to be very careful. My business also has many international clients; about 15 percent of our clients are companies from the Netherlands opening up their first US location. If there are cultural or language differences, it's especially important to choose your words carefully.

The cliff notes? When you feel reactive, sleep on it.

NAVIGATE THE CORNERS YOU CAN'T SEE AROUND

AS A BUSINESS OWNER, THERE'S UNCERTAINTY ON MY plate every single week. For example, Covid brought a tremendous amount of uncertainty in New York and around the world. Sometimes, you have to take a leap of faith in the face of uncertainty. Doing so requires heart. It's tempting to hang on to what we know simply because we feel a sense of control. However, I'm a big believer in the serenity prayer: "You must have the serenity to accept the things you cannot change, the courage to change the things you can, and the wisdom to know the difference." Or when all else fails, I go to the abbreviated serenity prayer that my friend Tom, a former priest from Ireland, introduced me to: "Fuck it!"

In addition to my insurance and expert witnessing business,

there has also been uncertainty in *family* business. After Dad died, I now help to manage my mother's finances and navigate the complex financial situation around the trust and family farm. There was a lot to learn, even though he and I had taken the time to sit down and prepare for the transition.

The week before he passed, he even commented to me how much work I would have to take on. I said I understood but had learned from the best. I had some faith and certainty in what he'd taught me.

So many of my cousins, my dad's nieces and nephews, say WWRD—what would Roger do? My cousin Pat said when Covid started, his mother was in an assisted living facility, so he asked himself what Uncle Roger would do. He realized my dad would take her out of the facility and bring her home until it was safe, so that's what he did. We carry around the lessons my dad taught us, which give us a way to face uncertainty.

KEEP IT SIMPLE

MY DAD WAS GREAT AT BREAKING COMPLEX IDEAS AND processes down so that people could understand them. One way this showed up in my life when I was young, especially, was that I always seemed to have a class project that would require a presentation. Now, I was never the "book smart" kid in the house; I was the street smart kid who was clever enough to save my ass when I was in a bind. But if I'm to be honest, it was something that always hit my self-esteem. One specific project that I worked on for Future Homemakers of America (FHA)—oh, how I can hear my NYC friends now—required a public speaking component. I remember working on it with my dad. He told me, "It's important to be understood, but it's more important not to be misunderstood."

This seems like such a basic concept, but its implications are vast. To this day, I return to this wisdom almost weekly. It particularly comes into play with my expert witness work.

When I started, my dad advised me to be careful not to make people feel stupid. Jargon and acronyms make people feel like they don't know what you're talking about. When I look at risk for a client, I always ask them to give me a layman's description of their business operations as if they were talking to their five-year-old nephew—no acronyms, no industry knowledge, just laying it all out in the simplest form.

When it comes to work—and life in general—trying to impress people with what you know is not nearly as important as being clear and kind. And as my Aunt Karen taught me back in high school, why use a ten-dollar word when you can use a nickel one?

HAVE STRETCH IN YOUR LIFE

WHEN I MOVED TO NEW YORK, MY DAD TOLD ME I HAD to find the University of Missouri alumni chapter because I'd have an instant connection with those people. I wouldn't have to explain where I was from; they'd just get it, and it would help me create community in a new place.

I reached out to the chapter, and no one got back to me for a long time. A few years later, I got an email from a friend of mine from college, Misty Jackson. She'd since moved to New York and become the president of the alumni chapter. I got involved and joined the local board before serving on the national board of directors. New York is a hot place with wealthy alumni, and there are various dinners and meet-and-greets.

While on the board, I received an invitation to a dinner with the then-chancellor of the University of Missouri, Brady Deaton, and his wife Anne, who is exceptionally accomplished in her own right. There are people in your life who make you pause. When they talk, you want to listen because they're so giving of their wisdom. Anne has been one of those people for me.

Plenty of people worry about dressing properly or using the right fork if the chancellor comes to dinner, but not me. I'm someone who's never been intimidated by status. People are people. Part of that ease, I believe, is why I instantly connected and hit it off with the pair of them at dinner. They've become a great part of my life for the last ten years.

Anne—who has been active in a women's mentoring group called Griffith's—recruited me to join. I made many important connections in this work. And, more importantly, developed lifelong friendships.

I leaned on that mentorship—and all Anne had taught me—specifically when I was approached to move through the chairs and ultimately be the national president of the group Women in Insurance & Financial Services (WIFS). I'd been on their board for some time, but being the president seemed like a huge jump. At first, I was very resistant. I am more of a "vice president" kind of woman. Even though both roles are important, it feels too scary to be the president because I don't want to take on too much—even though I end up doing more.

This offer scared me and felt like a big deal. I'd be the youngest national president in the over eighty-year history of the organization. I'd be the leader of women old enough to be my mother. I called Anne and explained the situation. I didn't know if I was the right person or what the right decision would be.

"You always have to have stretch in your life," she told me. "If you don't, you cease to exist. You always need something bigger than you because that's where you grow and develop character."

When she gave me that advice, it resonated with me. I'm an information gatherer. I have a good gut for quick decisions, but something that will impact others prompts me to take my time and do my research. I interviewed seven past presidents of the organization about their experience, time commitment, meaning, pitfalls, and lessons. I talked to Anne again, and then I ultimately decided to say yes.

This book is a stretch for me too. I'm very WYSIWYG, but in conversation. Putting stories on paper for posterity feels more consequential than an Instagram story that will disappear in twenty-four hours. I've had to grow into being more comfortable with telling people about working on this project. I'm generally comfortable talking about myself, but this journey stretches me to the next level. My biggest fear is the work wouldn't impact anyone.

As women, we go to the worst-case scenario. When I asked myself what the worst case would be as national president, I pictured shooting my mouth off in an interview and causing all the chapters to close down. I imagined someone taking out an ad in *The New York Times* about how much I suck, losing all my clients, and ending up selling fruit on the street. My husband doesn't go through those thought processes, but a lot of my girlfriends do.

My time in the organization has taught me how to pick a mentor and the value of peer-to-peer mentorships. Peer relationships are huge. I have several, including two friends, Juli and Kris, in Wisconsin who are also in insurance. (Remember the beginning of the book where I gave you my F-word rules...that's from them.) We all are in different sectors, but they are fantastic for bouncing ideas if I have business questions. They're level-headed, and they know me. Regular mentors might not call you out on your shit, but peers will because they see who you really are as a person. There are similarities to a close friendship but with the added layer of shared professional experience.

When Anne gave me advice, I was already ambitious and had a growth mindset, but I still needed to hear that, and I needed to hear it from someone I trusted. When you find a mentor like that, there isn't any challenge you can't tackle because your corner is never empty.

IF YOU DON'T VALUE YOUR TIME, NO ONE ELSE WILL

I HAD AN ENTREPRENEURIAL MOTHER FROM A VERY young age. My mom opened a Merle Norman cosmetics studio in 1987, and then she eventually had a travel agency. I'd work in her store after school, helping with inventory and gift wrapping. When I got older, she taught me how to do makeovers because she figured it would be a good skill to make some money while I went to college if I ever needed to.

Through those experiences, she learned about time management. Especially as a travel agent before the days of Expedia, if you built someone a beautiful itinerary and then they decided to do something else, you'd just wasted your time. She was in the travel agency business during the time when airlines stopped paying commissions on tickets, so she started charging servicing fees when she put packages together because she knew she needed to be paid for her time. As a kid, I learned that lesson from her: if you don't value your time, no one else will.

I took that lesson with me to New York, which lives and dies by networking. Expanding your network of salespeople and business owners is key. About five years into working for myself, I really started seeing my mom's point about valuing my time. I thought about what I was worth per hour. Any business owner or salesperson needs to know their hourly worth when they give their time to someone else.

How much does the time you spend cost you? I know I'm worth about $274 per hour, so if I have coffee to network with someone, what will I sell later that makes up for the $274? Am I just having coffee and giving free advice, or will that person lead me to business opportunities and more client referrals?

I've also learned not everyone has the same work ethic. I treat the volunteer and networking time in my calendar as business. If I commit to a meeting, I'll be there. Other people don't have that mindset, though, and they'll cancel at the last minute or bump those engagements for paid business. If people flake on me, it is perceived that they're saying they think their time is more valuable than mine.

At my office, anytime I have a networking meeting, my staff always asks people where they're coming from and schedules my meetings based on where I'm coming from to find a midway point between the two locations. It doesn't make sense to travel an hour each way when we could be more intentional about where and when we schedule meetings. That strategy has been successful for me because it saves the person I'm networking with and me time. We can find a coffee shop that works for both of us or whatever the case may be. That simple acknowledgment of where they're coming from expresses that I value their time.

I'm respectful of others' and my time, so I don't have much patience for people who disrespect my time. I have a "three strikes and you're out" rule. I know everyone encounters emergencies or extenuating circumstances sometimes. However, if flaking becomes a pattern, I won't waste my time again. If someone reschedules three times, I'll never meet with them. Some people might say that's harsh, but I value myself and set boundaries accordingly.

Of course, there are different uses of time, mainly revenue-generating and relational. Sometimes, I get speaking fees for conferences, and sometimes, I consciously decide to waive the fees and just get expenses if I know the engagement will lead to other revenue-generating opportunities or professional development. Other interactions are purely for enjoyment and don't have to be transactional. Not every coffee has to lead to business, but if the intent is networking, then both sides should respect each other's time.

The best way to figure out how much you're worth per hour is to calculate what you make per year, track how many hours you work per week, multiply those hours by fifty-two weeks, and then divide your total salary or revenue by the total hours. Once you have that concrete number, use it to guide your decisions. When you have a sense of your worth, it will shift your perspective about what is and isn't a good use of your time.

"DON'T SELL YOURSELF TO THE DEVIL TO GET TO THE NEXT LEVEL."

MY FRIEND AND COLLEAGUE COLLEEN BLUM FOUND me through a Google search of successful women in insurance. She'd been in a position that wasn't a good fit for her as a strong woman, so she decided to change her situation. She emailed the office, and we decided to meet for lunch. She was truly looking for mentorship and didn't ask for a job, but her initiative and drive impressed me. I knew I had an account manager going out on maternity leave, and I asked her if she'd be interested in filling in.

The rest is history. She's been working at my company for over seven years and became a partner on January 1st, 2021. She's a truly remarkable woman.

Over the years, we've become close. I learned that she started as a hair stylist before falling into the insurance world. She recognized she was in the wrong culture and took it upon herself to see what else was out there. I'm so fortunate she came along when she did. She recently spoke on a panel at the BenefitsPro Broker Expo, a conference we attended, and all these men around me said they were going to steal her, and I said they could go ahead and try. We have different ways of processing challenges and information, which is great. She calls me out on my shit, and I trust her deeply.

Our mentorship relationship has grown and evolved, and she now mentors *me* in ways she probably doesn't even realize. She can read my face, and she even tells new hires to watch for the sign when they should stop talking.

One of the most memorable things Colleen has shared with me is not to sell yourself to the devil to get to the next level. She learned this from seeing what goes on in our industry and others. We always laugh when we go to conferences and vendors lead with the commission we'll get. That approach turns us off because we believe if you do the right thing for the client, the money will come. In general, men in the industry want to know the commissions first, whereas many women in the industry have other motivations. We don't want to sell our souls for an extra few thousand dollars.

Especially in sales, dollar amounts are important, but we

don't want to compromise our morals or our ethics. I watch women who are cool with everything and flirt and hang with the men in our industry, while others get labeled as prudes because they don't take shit. Running my business has taught me the importance of learning to navigate those situations. Younger women in business can check their morals and ethics at the door if it means an opportunity, so I encourage people to understand there are other ways, which requires a confidence shift.

I've encountered questionable situations, which I'm sure relates to the fact my industry is only 14 percent women. It happens less now than it did when I was twenty-six. I carry myself in a certain way, and people know that I'll call them out. At the end of the day, I own my own company. I don't have to answer to a paycheck or a boss, which offers a tremendous amount of freedom instead of leaving me feeling stuck.

Even the way Colleen found me shows the value of a growth mindset, seeking out mentorship, and learning to navigate difficult situations. She's tenacious, which is one of the main qualities we look for in new hires: she always has the ability to find the answer. We want self-starters. If your path isn't what you want, how can you change it? In fact, Colleen started a podcast called *Try and Stop Me*. She loves what she does but wanted a creative outlet and to help other women coming up to advocate for themselves. Now, she's mentoring others, which is what the process is all about. Someone helped you, so now you help someone else. Everyone gets a leg up from someone.

You may be afraid to seek out more formal mentorship relationships, but I encourage you to admit when you need guidance, be vulnerable, and ask. Shoot your shot. The first person you ask might say no, but there are people out there who want to help. I'm one of them.

SPREAD YOUR WINGS, SLAY SOME DRAGONS

I THINK IT'S COMMON FOR YOUNG WOMEN TO BORROW someone else's identity until we figure out what our own is. Maybe because of social media and other societal changes, kids figure themselves out sooner than I did. I also had parents who helped me see the world was bigger than my backyard. I had permission to spread my wings to go slay some dragons as well as to come home if I wanted to.

It can be scary striking out on your own. I left Missouri for New York City without a job. I rolled the dice, but I also had a conversation with my parents. I knew I had a backup job in Detroit or New Orleans, but I wanted to try for my dream. My parents were gracious and believed in me. My dad and I talked about my trying for a month. I graduated at a good time in the job market, in 2001, so I had a plan, experience, and eight job offers—and then, for the last part, I took a leap of faith.

I always advise young people graduating from college to get the diploma, yes, but also to get the experience that can set them apart from their peers, especially in a tough job market. I know having work experience opened more doors for me and made striking out on my own a greater possibility.

MAKE YOUR SPENDING COUNT

I BELIEVE IN LIVING BELOW YOUR MEANS. NOBODY wants to work forever, so it's important to save. You can't buy everything you want and as my grampa Jerry taught me, "You never see a U-haul following a hearse." But you can start developing your future lifestyle through the choices you make today. I know people with car payments of $1,000-plus a month, which only holds them back. Choose your expenditures wisely and figure out what you truly desire that will have meaning for you and not just be an expensive want.

My dad and I were hunters. Whether I need a car or a dress, I spend time doing my research and finding the right one. I will try on fifty black dresses until I find the perfect one, and I never have buyer's remorse as a result. I don't want to buy something and then wish I'd bought something different or more affordable. I go searching for exactly what I need instead of falling into instant gratification.

Truly wealthy people often live below their means and amass wealth by not getting roped into keeping up with the Joneses. Real wealth also comprises more than money; it's also about relationships, family, humility, and keeping your finger on the pulse of life and what's truly important, my cousin Mike taught me that.

KNOW THE DIFFERENCE BETWEEN GETTING AHEAD AND BEING FULFILLED

WHEN YOU EVALUATE DIFFERENT OPPORTUNITIES, particularly in your career, look at the nonmonetary value of what you'll get. The place offering $10,000 more or a signing bonus might have an associated cost. Sometimes, it's good to make less money and have a better quality of life.

At my company, we close early on Fridays between Memorial Day and Labor Day. People can spend more time with their families around the holidays and work from home when they want to. We offer professional development to help people be their best and formalize mentorship relationships. Those aspects don't have a line item on a paycheck, but it's important to consider their value.

There are 168 hours in a week. If you spend fifty-six hours a week sleeping and forty to fifty working, then it's important to make sure what you do for work fulfills you. Yes, there are basic monetary requirements everyone needs to meet, but beyond that threshold, there's a huge difference between a job and a career. When people interview with me, I always ask whether they're looking for a job or a career. If they're looking for a job, I tell them to keep looking because this is an industry that requires real alignment with the path to succeed.

I started in crappy jobs and chose a low-paying position to build my career. I knew what I'd been doing before wasn't who I wanted to be for the rest of my life, but I had to step back and look at my motivation. I encourage you to do the same: are you following fulfillment or just biding your time? I learned how to make ends meet by being a personal trainer to supplement my income, but it was because I believed in myself and my career path that I was able to truly make a leap. Once I started building my client list, I could give up the job as a trainer, and then I truly started to flourish in my chosen career.

In my industry, we joke that no one says they want to be an

insurance broker when they grow up. You either fall into it or your family is in it. We say insurance isn't sexy, but our clients are. That said, it's a great industry for women. You get to educate people about policies and risk. You get to collaborate to find the best solution. I'm a fixer, and at the end of the day, I get to channel my superhero complex into solving problems for people. I can find the best policy to give them peace of mind. I'm also a strategist, and I have a reputation for being able to insure the weird and unusual. We're working with a company right now that makes robots, and it's a fascinating problem to solve for them.

This industry allows me to make my own destiny. People often talk about how women make seventy cents or less on the dollar compared to what men make, but when you work on commission, you make the same amount as the men. At the end of the day, I get that pay equity. There's no glass ceiling; it's already been shattered. Sometimes, people stereotype and want a woman broker because they think they'll get better customer service, which works in my favor too.

I'm motivated by money and make a very good living. I also work tremendously hard for it. I see a massive amount of opportunity for women in this industry. I encourage them to get in at the right time, though, so they can build their careers before they're married with kids and people are depending on them. In that sense, I was fortunate to start a firm when I was twenty-six, when I didn't have people depending on me for money. I had enough to take care of myself.

Sometimes career-changing works. I've seen retired teachers with pensions take up insurance as a second career. If you can get in early and make it work, even better. You get to meet so many different kinds of people and learn about different businesses, expanding your horizons. You can find opportunities to join advisory boards because of your expertise in risk management.

If you find yourself stuck on the career front, odds are that you're engaging in some form of negative self-talk about *why* you can't succeed. Challenge yourself to look back on your history and ask where that voice comes from. Why can't you do what you want to do now? What is it in you telling you that you can't? Rewrite your own story. It can take you far.

LIFT UP OTHER WOMEN

CAROLINE FEENEY IS THE CEO OF INSURANCE AND retirement businesses for Prudential. When I was on the national board for Women in Insurance & Financial Services, she was a keynote speaker for us. The insurance industry is mostly male, and there are even fewer women in leadership. We're talking single digits. She was very candid about her experiences as a woman in this industry—experiences that I believe can speak to how things work beyond the world of insurance.

In her speech, Caroline talked about two types of women: the ones always reaching back to help pull you up behind them—like mentors or sponsors within a company who help you advance—and the ones clawing at you from behind as you rise to the top. You can see and feel that visual. We've all experienced both types, I'm sure. Think about it: you know some women you wouldn't piss on if they were on fire, and you know lots of wonderful ones. I do too.

When I worked in hospitality, I had the opportunity to fill in as a corporate sales manager at a hotel in Columbia, Missouri. The front desk manager had worked her way up, and she felt threatened by any woman who might rise into a leadership opportunity. She didn't see room at the table for another woman; she saw me as competition, even though it was a temporary role. She'd purposely schedule me to be in the front desk right after my corporate sales role. I wore a suit for the corporate role, but once I didn't have time to go home and change into my uniform for the desk shift. She sent me home to change.

She didn't want anyone looking at me in a suit and thinking I might be in charge. It was a power trip. I still remember how unnecessary that dynamic felt. She could have talked to me about bringing my uniform with me next time, but instead she humiliated me in front of my peers and coworkers. That experience showed me I never wanted to be like her as a boss or board member. I never wanted to cut someone down to make myself feel bigger because people who act that way ultimately just look like assholes and don't realize it. She taught me not all women play well together in the sandbox. A male manager never would have cared, let alone sent me home.

That experience helped shape the kind of company culture I wanted to have. My partner Colleen works *with* me, not *for* me, and I correct people who say otherwise. It's an intentional mindset. You can see people flourish when you cultivate that difference in an office. If you're in a place of leadership, give people (women especially) the credit they deserve and encourage them to feel ownership over the work. This comes back to two lessons I've been hammering since the beginning of this book: remember where you come from, and nobody gets anywhere on their own. As women, we have the opportunity to lift up other women not in competition to us, but beside us.

More of that, please.

THE SYRUP

- Don't ask someone to do something you wouldn't do yourself. I was an event manager at the University of Missouri, and on show days, we'd have a staff of 200 or more people. I always got respect from the staff because I'd work right alongside them setting up chairs, moving heavy items, or otherwise participating in the thick of it. That way, they saw I was capable of the tasks, but we could achieve more as a team. That approach keeps me humble and connected to where I came from.

- Instead of being reactive, sleep on it. Trust me.

- In my insurance business, I still know how to do the different tasks that I delegate. If someone is out, I can step in and fill in for those roles. Doing so keeps my finger on the pulse of every aspect of the business and keeps me connected to the people around me.

- Figure out how much you're worth per hour and have a conscious thought process around who and what you spend your time on based on that value.

- Recognize the difference between transactional versus relational time spent and their respective values.

- If you have to talk yourself into something, it's better to pass on it.

- Pursue fulfillment and know your skills. My tendency to game out the worst-case scenario works great for me in this industry.

- In terms of compensation, especially as a woman, know your worth and how you deserve to be compensated. Start by calculating your worth per hour. If someone asks you to grab coffee but you don't want to, you can turn them down more easily if you know it will take you an hour and a half total, costing you $300 of your time, not just $5 for the coffee. That calculation is why I don't take unscheduled phone calls. Time is money. I can call people back later or make exceptions for paying clients, but I have that profit-and-loss calculation in my mind.

FINAL THOUGHTS

WHATEVER YOUR EXPERIENCE OF LOSS OR STRIFE OR challenges in life, I encourage you never to be scared to share your story with people. When you do, it not only serves as catharsis for you, but it can also make a difference for someone else going through a difficult time. The same goes for your wisdom and the wisdom you've gathered over the years: share it, and its impact grows.

That's what I hope I've done here, at least a little. I hope you've gained some perspective and motivation in these stories. As I said when we began, if you don't have a great mentor in your life, I invite you to let this book be your mentor until you secure a person to help you. I hope you'll also feel called to mentor other people and stop questioning whether you're qualified enough. I'm sure you have something to teach. A quick way to tell is that if people ask you for advice—you're doing something right.

I encourage you to always remember that there's a difference between hearing and listening. The advice in this book comes from times I've paused and listened to other people instead of thinking about myself and what I want to say next. Sometimes, you have to stop the noise in your head and stop multitasking, so you can be fully present. This can be hard for women, I know. But it's worth it.

There's also a difference between listening and implementing. And not all you've read will make sense to implement right now. Like I said when we started this adventure together, this book is not one-size-fits-all advice. The point isn't for every experience I've had to resonate with you but rather to share the gifts of advice I've received.

I hope reading has sparked memories of advice you've learned along the way. What do you have to share with someone else? What do you wish you'd known when you were younger? Who could use that knowledge now? Who can you pass this book to? Who needs lifting up?

In thinking this way, you're modeling Roger. You're good when nobody is looking. And you just might be surprised by how uplifted you feel in the process.

A REMINDER TO SLOW DOWN

I WILL LEAVE YOU WITH THIS STORY, ONE THAT STILL makes me smile to this day.

As a former helicopter pilot, my dad used to joke that he had "a speedometer in his pants." He could always tell you within two miles an hour how fast you were driving.

When I was in high school, my brother and I had been at a wedding dance a couple of towns over. (In the Midwest, people go to those dances when they're not invited, and it's not really considered wedding crashing. Certain receptions are more "open invitations" to the community. My friends in New York don't understand this, which is always a funny thing to try and explain, but it's how I grew up.)

Matt and I had gone in separate vehicles and needed to

get home for curfew. On my way home, I got pulled over. Not for drinking, but for speeding. I was always a polite kid and very respectful, so of course I didn't give the officer any grief. I *knew* I was speeding just a little in order to get home in time. Plus, and maybe more importantly, giving grief wouldn't have done any good. People knew who my dad was because he was a judge.

I apologized to the officer, and he let me go with a warning. When I got home, I was late for curfew. As I was leaning over the bathroom sink washing my face and brushing my teeth, I heard my dad from the stairs that lead straight up to my bedroom. I'll never forget it.

"Little late, little girl."

I knew I couldn't lie to him about why I was late because he'd find out the truth at the courthouse, so I admitted I'd gotten pulled over. I *did* lie about the speeding, though, because I was still a kid in many ways, and I didn't want to disappoint my dad.

"The officer told me I was going sixty-seven miles an hour, but that's not possible," I told him. "I had my cruise control set."

"Your speedometer could be off, which could have kicked you over sixty-five." That was the threshold for pulling people over. We both knew it. "After church tomorrow, you and I are going for a ride."

I was nervous, of course, but I had no choice but to agree.

"And that speedometer had better be off," he said.

I was sweating. I didn't want to get in trouble, sure. But I was a lot more concerned about disappointing my dad. Even as a dumb teenager who made mistakes, I still held him in such high regard.

The next day after church, we went for a drive. Somehow, judging by the speedometer in his pants, my dad determined that mine really *was* off by two miles an hour. Whether it truly was or whether he was giving me one of countless lessons on forgiveness, love, family, second chances, and doing the right thing...I still can't tell.

"Now you know, though," he told me, warmth in his eyes, "so don't forget it."

I haven't forgotten, Dad. Or anything else you taught me. And now, all of those things can help other people who are reading this. And as a byproduct, this book will help your fellow veterans you cared for so deeply. I think we did good. I hope you are enjoying your pancakes. You deserve them.

ACKNOWLEDGMENTS

To **my husband Sean**: You love me when I'm unloveable. There is no one else I'd rather do life with than you. I promise to always have your six, even if I suck at loading the dishwasher and my aura is too loud.

To the **Veterans Clinic**: Thank you for being such an inspiration and impacting so many lives for both our veterans and their families. The work you do is immense.

To the **Breakfast Club**: You have been my "small town" in NYC. The love and support you have given me for nearly twenty years has been unwavering. I have learned to be a grown-up and how to do life on life's terms with your guidance.

To the **Cool Kids Lunch Table**: You are all irreplaceable. I'm so glad to have you as part of my framily!

To the **Wonder Woman Crew**: I didn't know how much joy you ladies would bring into my life. You all inspire me every day to think outside the box and strive for more.

To the **Combs Crew**: thank you for keeping the wheels on the bus when my life gets chaotic!

To the **Dutch Kills Crew**: You all came into my life when I needed it most. You keep me sane, healthy, and coming back for more bench presses!

To the **community of King City**: I'll always be a Missouri chick at heart. Thank you for helping raise me and being part of the foundation that my home and heart are built upon.

To **my mentors**: This book wouldn't be possible if it wasn't for you all. Thank you for bestowing your wisdom on me so that I can pay it forward.

To the **Scribe Team**: This project couldn't have been done without you. I will forever be thankful for this journey we have had together and the people you have brought into my life.

To **my girls**: I couldn't do this life without you. Our bonds transcend time, space, and distance. But always remember,

I'm just like a candle...if you forget about me, I'll burn your house down!

To **my mentees** I have had throughout my life: you make me strive for greatness, all the while teaching me more than you'll ever know. You have all made me proud and are more amazing than you realize.

To **my family**: I know we are a little bit loud and a little bit crazy, but we've sure got a whole lot of love. Thank you for letting me do things in my own way and letting me know I can always come home.

To **my friends**: thank you for not being ugly and not being assholes.

To **Dad**: My most honorable role in my life is being your daughter. Thank you for always believing in me.

ABOUT THE AUTHOR

 **SUSAN L. COMBS** is President of Combs & Company, a full-service insurance brokerage firm based in New York City. Susan founded the business when she was only twenty-six years old and has built her company on the concept of "Do more, better." She also takes this message to the companies she advises and the developing leaders she mentors. From 2014–2015, Susan was named the National President of Women in Insurance & Financial Services (WIFS)—the youngest to hold that role in the organization's eighty-five-plus year history. Susan is especially proud to have received the Graduate Of the Last Decade (G.O.L.D) Award from the University of Missouri in 2011, to have been recognized as the first female to receive the Broker Of the Year (BOY) Award by BenefitsPro Magazine, and to have received WIFS' highest honor: Woman of the Year. In addition, Susan's expertise in the complexities of

health insurance has made her a sought after expert witness, advisor, and speaker.

With all that said, at heart, Susan will tell you she's "just a Missouri girl in a New York world."

She prides herself on "making it" in New York City but remains true to her Midwestern roots as her late father Roger—a former Two-Star General and circuit judge—taught her.

Today, Susan lives in Queens with her husband, Sean, and their four-legged "kids" Pepper and Roxy. An avid athlete, Susan enjoys pushing herself and building community at her beloved Dutch Kills CrossFit and Strongman gym. When she's not flipping colossal tires or rocking the world of insurance, Susan actively supports the University of Missouri School of Law Veterans Clinic and is a hospice volunteer.

Whenever possible, she travels to her hometown of King City, Missouri (population 1,013) to visit with her mom, a former entrepreneur. Susan's oldest brother, David, works in IT in Kansas; her middle brother, Matt, is a hospice RN in Missouri, and resides in St. Joseph, MO, with his wife Joan and their daughters Josie and Evie.